LONG HOT SUMMER
By
IAN SNOWBALL

FOR ISABEL (1969-2010)

This book is dedicated to Mum, Dad, Nita, Mart and my Josie.

First Edition published September 2011 by Heavy Soul Records
Second Edition published October 2011 by Heavy Soul Records
www.heavysoul45s.co.uk
Text copyright 2011 Ian Snowball.
ISBN 978-0-9570559-0-2
Cover photograph kindly supplied by Stuart Deabill.

Contents layout by Ian Snowball and Adam Cooper.

All song titles quoted in this book are for the purposes review, study or criticism.

Characters are fiction and any resemblance to any living soul is simply a strange coincidence.

This story was only possible because of my friends whom I am proud of and feel indebted to.
Thank you fellas

Special thanks to The Jam and The Style Council, my mentor Pete McKenna, Whole Point publications for the opportunity and the 1980's. Also the small words of encouragement that helped things along from the likes of Paolo Hewitt (especially his carousel story), John King, Mark' Bax' Baxter (a salt of the earth geeza) and Adam of Heavy Soul for the support and belief. Keep on keeping on Adam!

Cover photo courtesy of a younger Stuart Deabill.

4

LONG HOT SUMMER

'If you was a teenage boy during the 1980's then this is your story not mine'

'I fucking hope my mum remembered to get another gas bottle for the drinks machine,' cried Robert, as pieces of the pickled onion flavoured crisps that he was chewing sprayed all over his walking companion.

'For fucks sake,' complained Loz, dusting the crumbs off of his polo shirt.

'Sorry mate,' apologised Robert, then continued 'Hey, hold on a minute will yer, I've got something in my shoe!'

Loz crossed his arms and watched on as Robert squashed the empty crisp bag into the pocket of his black sta-prest trousers. He fumbled around inside his pocket for a moment before adding, 'Here, hold this too.'

Loz took the record that Robert handed him. It was The Specials *'Specials'* album. Robert then plonked himself down on the grassy floor and removed one of his loafers. Loz noticed a blood stain on Roberts white flannel sock.

'Got a blister have you?' he asked.

'Yeah, and it fucking hurts. Mind you it's my own fault really; these loafers were not the best choice of footwear for a school sponsored walk were they.'

Loz just nodded in agreement. He felt quite smug in his comfortable desert boots. Robert adjusted his sock with a wince then replaced his shoe. Loz extended his hand to help him get back on his feet. Robert stood up and brushed some dry grass from off his trousers. Robert was slightly taller than Loz and had messy brown hair with a side parting. He looked good in his loafers, sta's and tee-shirt in the colours of his favoured football team, West Ham United. Loz had fair hair with a left side parting. He had freckles over his nose and piercing blue eyes that girls would often comment on. The two school friends continued to walk together soaking in the sunshine and smell of recently cut grass. They looked similar in their polo shirts and sta's. Only their footwear set them apart from their fashion leanings. Loz was a Mod, whereas Robert was a Rude Boy.

It was a hot sunny day for the school's annual sponsored walk. The boys walked six miles in all, which was only achieved by trudging several laps of the school playing field. The whole school was involved so every pupil turned out for the occasion in their best togs. Nobody had to wear their school uniform on sponsored walk day, and having the permission to wear what they wanted contributed to the excitement of the event.

Loz and Robert walked at a steady pace. They were in no rush to exit the school gates at 3.20 for their very last time.

'It don't feel real, does it?' remarked Robert. Loz understood what he was referring to.

'Not really, no. If I'm going to be honest, I've been trying to avoid thinking about it' replied Loz.

'I know, I'm kacking it. I've had my mum, dad and gran reminding me constantly for weeks that the final day of school was just around the corner.'

'Well it's not exactly your final day is it' interjected Loz, and then continued 'you're going to the grammar ain't you?'

'Well yeah, that's if I stay. I'm still in two minds about the whole grammar school thing and i can see me walking out after a few weeks'. Robert groaned.

'Fuck off will you. Your dad would go fucking mental, he would never allow it. Your destiny is mapped out mate, you're gonna turn up at the grammar school on your first day with a dozen certificates tucked under your arm, then, a couple of years later you'll turn up at some shitty university with a load of O Levels tucked under your other arm, then you'll spend the next three of four years learning some old bollocks about socialism or something and then get a cushy job that pays well. Following that it will be a nice three bedroom house in one of the rural villages outside of town, wife, kids, new car and a shirt and tie for everyday for the next forty years.'

Robert assessed what Loz had said but remained silent. Loz was not sure if his description of his companion's future had pleased him or hurt him. He decided to change the subject and referred to The Specials album.

'I don't have a copy of this.' He said as he ran his eyes over the album cover. Loz liked the simplicity of the use of black and white imagery that made its direct link to the essence of the Two Tone ethos.

'They were a good looking band, The Specials,' he commented.

'Yeah, look great don't they in their pork pie hats and loafers' returned Robert enthusiastically.

'My favourite picture of The Specials is the photograph of them on the cover of 'Do Nothing'. I think they look brilliant in their moccasins and tartan trousers. It's a really good look; I wonder if it was a look adopted by the suit wearing Rude Boys up north.'

Loz was nodding thoughtfully, and then handed Robert the album that he had been carrying. It was 'Sound Affects' by The Jam.

'Thanks,' replied Robert.

The two of them had agreed to bring with them a copy of their favourite album to date so that the other could borrow it. The two friends had built their relationship on sharing their tastes in music.

'I got that for one of my birthdays.' Begun Loz, 'I had asked for it so was no surprise when I got it from my mum and dad. Mind you, even though I knew I was getting it, I

6

was still thrilled and after having torn the wrapping off I played the album over again and again. I remember that birthday really clearly. I also got a pair of wrap rounds too and some money. I remember wandering off into town by myself. I went to Woolies and bought a copy of the 'That's Entertainment' single with its Pinkish picture cover. You know the one using similar imagery and colours as the Sound affects album. German import you know. It cost me fifty pence. Thing was when I got home I found the single did not have one of them plastic bits that go in the middle so I had to walk all the way back into town to get one.'

Robert chuckled then assured Loz that he would play the record that night and Loz agreed that he would play the Specials album in return.

'Good luck Robert, good luck Lawrence,' belted the voice from Mr Woolson, one of the P.E teachers. He walked past them at pace dressed in a Slazenger tracksuit and a whistle swinging from around his neck.

'And you,' replied Robert.

'How many miles have you got left?' shouted Loz knowing that Mr Woolson had decided to walk ten miles instead of the six. He prided himself on 'outdoing' his pupils.

'Three.' Mr Woolson yelled back, 'I'll be done in time to see you off at the school gates though.'

Loz had liked Mr Woolson, and for a moment actually felt like he may miss him. He then recalled the times he had seen Mr Woolson lose his temper and throw the black board rubber at the offending pupil. Loz had never been on the end of one, but had witnessed many being thrown. On a few occasions if no black board rubbers were available, Mr Woolson would throw his bunch of keys instead. The sight of the large collection of keys hurtling through the air towards an unsuspecting child's head was a frightful sight. Nevertheless Loz realised these were the sort of things he would miss.

'What are you going to miss about this place?' he asked Robert.

Robert thought for a moment then said, 'Sports lessons I suppose, cricket on the top field mostly, biology lessons too, just because of old Pilton, that teacher is a loon, and of course dribbling over the sight of Miss Yeldings tits and arse.' Loz laughed and agreed then added.

'Yeah, I'll miss her too. I've always had a thing for Miss Barter as well, it's a shame she did not want to risk losing her job and give me a good seeing to in detention from time to time.'

The pair laughed and fantasised as they continued to walk in the sweltering heat.

The smell of Patchouli oil wafted over them as they were over taken by three other pupils.

'I won't miss them bloody Greebos,' commented Robert.

Loz added, 'yeah, smelly meatheads,' taking the piss out of the clothing the pupils wore. They were dressed head to toe in denim, which were covered in patches of bands that advertised Deep Purple, AC/DC and Hawkwind.

'Scruffy, filthy bastards,' yelled Robert to which one of the 'Greebos' stuck his hand in the air gesturing a wanker sign as he continued to walk.

'Smelly bastards,' retorted Loz. All involved knew it was only playful banter. They had spent the past four years mocking each others taste in music. But at the end of the day they still happily shared classes with one another. All the rivalry between the various fashion groups over the years could only be light hearted fun. It was normal and it was expected the Mods mocked the Skinheads, the Skinheads the Meatheads, the Meatheads the Rude Boys, the Rude Boys the New Romantics and the New Romantics the Mods and around it went. Basically everyone else that did not dress like you or listen to the same music as you was a target. And everyone at school partook of the game. It was only outside in the streets and discos that the mocking and intolerance turned into violence and cat and mouse chases. The amount of violence the mouse or how many streets it had to run down depended on how big the cat was or how many others were in the cats group. Sometimes it was fun, but more often than not, it was just plain scary.

'What's the time?' asked Loz.

'Two,' replied Robert.

'Not long then, our last hour at school.'

'Are you going to the hall to say goodbye to the teachers?' enquired Robert.

'Fuck off, course not, why are you?'

'Yeah, I was going to. There are a few people I want to say goodbye to. I might not get the chance again.'

Loz knew that Robert was right and he was aware that something in him also wanted to go and formally say goodbye to the past four years of his life. He also knew that it was the thing only the squares and briefcases would did so he knew he would not be going to the hall to see the teachers and other pupils. Besides him and several other pupils had alternative plans as their way to say goodbye to the school. The thought of their plan excited him more than shaking hands with a teacher who probably did not really give a toss in truth.

Loz looked out over the school playing field at hundreds of other school children traipsing around. The young children sucked lollipops and sipped away at their cans of fizzy drinks and the older children walked with swaggers and a deceptive confidence. Some knew they would be walking through the school gates for the last time and into an unknown world. Most of them, if they could admit it felt nervous and scared.

Loz felt like the last hour dragged. As the final minutes of his last day at school approached he detected a mixture of excitement and anxiety deep inside himself. Gradually, groups of pupils and staff peeled away having completed their six miles. Even Mr Woolson had disappeared to the school hall to shake his sweaty hand with the squares.

Loz and Robert had said their goodbyes. Theirs was only temporary because they would be seeing each other again over the school holidays period. Loz had then made his way towards what was called the 'smokers' corner making sure he avoided the path that led to the school hall. He did not want a weak moment and find himself in the school hall participating in emotional farewells with the teachers, the squares and the meatheads. Once Loz arrived safely at the 'smokers' corner he was greeted with around a dozen friends.

One of them, Steve offered him a go on his cigarette. Loz refused. He had never smoked. Even though he had spent hundreds of hours in break times hanging around the smokers corner, he had managed to avoid falling prey to the 'cancer sticks'.

'Are you going tonight? Steve asked looking intently at Loz.

'Yeah, I'll get there about six, how about you?'

'About seven, I'm hoping my old man will give me and piggy a lift down,' he returned.

They were discussing the Howard Wardell Youth Club disco being held to celebrate the last day of school for many of its members. It was promising to be a special occasion, with a few of the older Mods providing the music.

'Do you think Steph and Theresa will come?' enquired Steve.

'I dunno, but yeah probably, I see no reason why they wouldn't, it's their last day of school too.'

Steve walked away grinning. He anticipated a possible snog and fingering session with Steph. Next thing there was some pushing and shoving to the sounds of yells and laughter. One of the boys had dropped his trousers to his ankles and was squatting near the floor.

'What the fuck are you doing you dirty sod?' asked another boy.

'I'm leaving the teachers a present.' replied the squatter.

The group backed away as the squatter delivered the goods. Then Steve signalled for the big moment. The whole group sensed the moment they had been waiting for had arrived and got excited.

'It's three twenty,' announced Steve as he removed his school blazer and tie from a plastic carrier bag. Another boy handed Steve a lighter and with an enormous grin on his face he began to set fire to the items. Tie first and then the blazer which caught fire quickly. The rest of the group joined in and one after the other every blazer and every tie was set ablaze.

Loz watched on intently as the school crest on his blazer breast pocket turned into ash. The moment lingered and then it was gone. The group had now swelled to about thirty boys. Mostly they just observed the funeral pyre of school regalia and then a few other items like books and P.E kits were added.

'Get out of my way, move boy, move it' roared Mr Woolson as he set about trying to contain the fire with one of the school's fire extinguishers. The group of boys laughed and applauded as their teacher of four years attacked the fire. Mr Woolson's face was bright red and he was sweating profusely.

In a matter of minutes it seemed the whole school had left the school hall and had come to witness the fiery revolutionary scene. The head teacher and the staff tried to control the mass of pupils but it was too chaotic for them. Mr Woolson managed to extinguish the fire and threw the empty extinguisher to the floor. His bright red, angry face then turned to the group of boys who stood laughing. He knew it was their blazers and ties that were now a pile of ashes on the school floor.

'You stupid pricks,' he addressed them all but looked directly at Steve whom he suspected had been the instigator. Steve simply gave Mr Woolson a cheeky wink. He knew he was now untouchable. No more detention, no more condescension, no more having to give a fuck. Steve then informed his group that it was time for them to leave and with a parting middle finger farewell to the teachers, cried out;

'I hope you have a long hot summer.'

Loz followed the exodus and without a single glance back each boy exited the green metal gates of the school for the very last time.

BOY ABOUT TOWN

Some of the group loitered at the shops near the school but Loz headed straight home. He had enjoyed setting the blazers and ties ablaze but now felt like he may regret not keeping the tie to show his children in the distant future. He felt slightly foolish. Once home, he said his hello's to his mum who was busy cooking sausage, mash and peas and ignored his older sister and younger brother. He ran up to his bedroom and gently placed the borrowed 'Specials' album beside his record player. He caught a glimpse of himself in the mirror and a smile grew onto his face as he reminded himself that he'd just left school for the last time. His sister interrupted the moment by barking up the stairs;

'Oi, mum said there's a package in her and dad's bedroom for you. It's from the catalogue.'

Loz did not shout anything back but bounced down the stairs to get the package. Brilliant timing, he thought to himself knowing full well what was contained in the package. He then returned to his bedroom which was located in the converted attic of the family four-storey home. By the time he had reached his bedroom he had already un-ceremonially ripped the plastic wrapping off of the package. A wide grin grew on his face as he held up the blue, yellow and white cycling shirt covered in advertising slogans. The shirt was a gift from his parents as a school leaving present. It also disguised the incentive for Loz to seek out and secure himself a job. Loz immediately fell in love with the shirt. He admired the use of colours and especially liked the way the round collar neck had a zipper. Loz pictured himself pulling the zipper up so that the collar rested under his chin thinking to himself that it would look the nuts. He carefully laid the shirt flat out on his bed and ran off towards the bathroom.

After a quick wash and brush up a splash of after shave and the sound of an old boxer's voice echoing in his mind he raced back to his bedroom. As he passed his sisters bedroom he yelled some abuse through the door at the Human League record she was prancing around to. Once he was back in his room he hastily slipped on a pair of his favourite army green combat trousers. He loved the way they tapered at the bottom and had built in zips. He had searched high and low for them eventually finding them in an army surplus store in a nearby town. Next he pulled some white socks over his feet and climbed into a grey tee shirt. Loz was still dressing himself as he ran back down the three flights of stairs to the kitchen. The kitchen was in the basement of the house. It had a large window that looked out into a small narrow court yard and then a thirty foot narrow garden with a shed standing like a small castle at the top of it.

Loz's mum and younger brother were sat at the family size wooden table and were half way through eating their tea. Loz searched the draining board for a glass and then filled it with water. As he turned he saw his brother pretending to push a pea up one of his nostrils. This made Loz and his mum chuckle. They remembered the time when he was much younger and had actually pushed a pea up his nose at the dinner table one day. Loz's dad had had to turn him upside down and shake the pea out of his nose. Everyone was convinced it came out of the other nostril. Ever since then the pea event had become a family joke and talking point.

'I've made you a gypsy tart that you can have after that' said Loz's mum nodding towards a plate full of sausages and mash potato. He picked up the plate of food and placed it on the table where he sat next to his mum. He sat close to the table to ensure he didn't drip any sausage fat onto his combats.

'How was your last day at school' enquired his mum.

'Was okay I 'spose. I finished the six miles and shook the hands of some of the teachers and even a couple of the okay briefcases too.'

'Briefcases?' questioned his mum looking confused.

'The squares, the straights,' butted in Loz's brother spitting out Brown sauce as he did so.

Loz's mum continued to ask him questions about his last day at school but he did not hear her. He was too busy wolfing down his meal and keeping an eye on the gypsy tart.

'Have you got a plan for the next few weeks?' asked his mum as she cut a thick slice from the gypsy tart and plonked it into an orange bowl.

Loz shoved a large spoonful of the tart into his mouth and mumbled 'yeah, have fun in the school holidays.'

His brother giggled as they mum looked over her shoulder from the sink area where she had begun washing up.

'Ah, but they are not school holidays for you any more are they Loz?'

The words grabbed Loz's attention. They hit hard. His mum was right. All of a sudden the sweet gypsy tart tasted bitter. Loz felt his upbeat mood change and drop a notch. His mum sensed the reaction.

'Look, what I suggest you do is enjoy yourself for a couple of weeks first. Give yourself time to adjust to the fact that you have now left school. Then after a couple of weeks go and find yourself a job. Your dad and I know it's not going to be easy but we have always said if you want a job you'll find a job. Why don't you look at Top Man or Burtons first? Isn't that what your friend Richard is doing?'

Loz grunted a yes to ensure her that he had heard her. He tried to finish the gypsy tart but could not manage it. Instead he pushed the bowl in the direction of his brother whose eyes sparkled at the thought of extra tart to consume. Loz walked back up the stairs with less spring in his steps. He could not even be bothered to hurl any further abuse at his sister's choice of music. Loz hardly noticed ABC was playing.

Once back in his bedroom he perched himself on the edge of his bed. He sat quietly reflecting on what his mum had said.

'Fucking hell,' he whispered, 'she's right, I'm never going to have another school holiday. Bollocks.'

Loz slid off the bed and onto his knees where he knelt beside his record player. To the left of the record player lived his record collection. An impressive collection of 45's, 12" and 33's that had been built up and added to for several years. Loz was not sure what he wanted to listen to. The collection reflected his participation in modernism. A mix of Northern Soul records mostly on the 'Kent' and 'Inferno' labels but with a fair amount of originals discovered at boot fairs. His prized boot fair find was Frankie Valli's *'The Night'*. Loz also had a respected collection of Stax, Motown and Atlantic releases as well. Alongside the Soul records mingled Ska and Reggae on 'Trojan' and 'Blue beat', again mostly boot fair finds. The main stream stuff on Two Tone and from bands like The Small Faces, The Who, The Yardbirds, Secret Affair were mainly purchased from local shops in the town. Loz's most prized collection however was from The Jam. He had virtually every record The Jam had ever released and this included German and Japanese imports.

Loz flicked slowly through the record collection until he paused at the Jam's *'Gift'* album. He gently removed the black oily record from the sleeve and balanced it carefully on the tips of his fingers. Loz then placed the record onto the record deck and set the machine in motion. He glanced down at the sleeve design. He had always liked the design. It was his second favourite next to the *'Sound Affects'* cover. He ran his eyes over the images of Weller, Foxton and Buckler and again wondered why they had been portrayed as a set of traffic lights. Buckler jogging on the spot in red, Foxton in amber and Weller, with cool shades on in green. Loz had often pondered if the green represented a new start 'Go', the red meant 'the end of The Jam', 'stop' and the amber signified the not sure where to go to next element.

The album started with Paul Weller yelling *'Babeeee'* followed by a pounding drum beat and then launching himself into *'Happy Together'*. Loz thought of his old school. Loz allowed the first verse and chorus to play but required something more upbeat and uplifting. He lifted the needle and placed it awkwardly where he wanted it. The *'Transglobal expresssssssssssssssssss'* hissed Weller – perfect. With its stomping Northern Soul style beat the song belted out of the speakers. He twisted the volume knob up slightly as Buckler whipped up a storm with his aggressive pounding of his drums. The beat kicked in and so did his spirit. He leapt to his feet and removed his 'Lonsdale' tee shirt which he threw onto the floor. He grabbed his new cycling shirt and pulled it over his head. It slipped over him with ease. He turned to spy himself in the wardrobes built in mirror. Loz ran his hands over the garment feeling its cotton texture. It felt smooth. He felt cool. He admired himself in the shirt in the mirrors reflection. It pleased him that the shirt and combats he wore complimented each other.

Next he approached his shoe collection. A jumbled pile of Jam shoes, loafers, deck shoes, and brogues of several different colours. He searched the pile for his blue and white slip on deck shoes. He found one but not the other and lost patience. Instead Loz opted for his white leather Adidas boxing boots with the red, white and blue stripes. He tied the laces and nodded his head in time with the drum beats. Then a final glance in the mirror to confirm the look and he left allowing the record player to turn itself off. On the way down the stairs The Jam faded and gave way to the poppy sounds from Culture club. This time he could not resist. As he passed his sisters bedroom he screamed through the door 'fucking poofs' and legged it.

Loz burst into the living room where he found his mum watching *Crossroads* and his brother flicking through the pages of a Doctor Who annual. They exchanged a few words and then Loz exited the room through the front door that opened up onto the street. The street was void of any life except a handful of the local cats that slept on car bonnets. The walk to the Howard Wardell youth club would only take five minutes. Not enough to build up a sweat. Loz was feeling good in himself again. The Jam had done the job, as usual. He knew he could rely on The Jam to lift his spirits. He was also excited about the disco he was heading for.

Loz passed the post office at the top of his road. It was still open because it also doubled up as a corner shop selling the usual sweets, milk, fags. There used to be another corner shop opposite but this had since turned into a video hire shop. As he walked past the post office he glanced inside. Mr Patel was looking vacant whilst stacking the shelves with loaves of bread. Loz waved at him but Mr Patel just looked at him blankly. Loz presumed his mind was concerned with shop matters. A little further along the street was the Dog pub which was a typical style pub, traditional inside and out. The landlord was famous, or at least had been in the sixties. He had been a bassist in a band who had had a number one record. Loz never liked the record but liked the fact that someone famous lived near him. Loz had also heard a rumour that David Bowie had at one time lived in the same street as the pub. But he never found out for certain if this rumour was true.

Loz passed the pub which had been closed since three o clock and crossed the main road. He strolled casually down the road which was on a hill. He took the opportunity to catch glimpses of himself in the reflections from the houses windows. He thought he looked good in his new cycling shirt. As he reached the alley way that led to the youth club he spotted a group of youths loitering half way along it. He recognized them instantly and felt safe. The group consisted of four of the older Mods from around town. Loz puffed his chest out and straightened his back as he approached them.

As he neared them one of the boys greeted him. This left Loz feeling privileged.

'Alright Loz' said the tallest boy in the group. He was dressed in a sky blue monkey jacket, jeans and black and blue bowling shoes. His hair was a recently trimmed French line. The lacquer glistened in the sunlight.

'Alright Den. I heard that you were doing some Dee Jaying tonight. Will you spin *'Out on the floor'* later for me?'

Den grinned and winked. 'Here you want a swig?'

He offered Loz the bottle of whiskey that he was clutching.

Loz had not yet acquired the taste of alcohol but did not have the guts to refuse in front of the older Mods. Loz knew all too well that reputations were built and destroyed on such matters. Loz accepted the bottle and disguised a moderate sip. He had to control himself from not spitting the fiery liquid all over the older Mods. He hoped his face was not going bright red. He felt that it should be. One of the other boys in the group slapped him on the back. He was only slightly taller than Loz and wore a denim jacket and jeans with deck shoes. Loz knew that he was leaving to join the Navy soon. The boy held his hand out to take the bottle from Loz and Loz handed it to him. The boy then took a swig and then passed it to one of the others in the group who replaced the bottle cap and stuffed the bottle deep into the pocket of his fish tail parka.

The group then set off from the alley and headed for the direction of the youth club entrance. Several young people hung around the entrance area. The bassy sound of music seeped from out of the club. It was unmistakeably *'Do the dog'* by The Specials.

'Spud is on the decks then,' commented the older mod who was off to join the Navy.

'Yep. He did say he was going to play loads of Ska tonight,' replied the parka wearing youth.

Loz was the first to reach the entrance and opened it allowing the older Mods to enter. Loz followed and was greeted by Dave, one of the youth club workers. Dave looked up with a grin and held one of his hands out. In the other hand he extinguished his fag. He blew out the last of his smoke through his nostrils.

'How much this time then Dave?' asked Loz.

'Same as the last time Loz, twenty pence.'

Loz riffled through one of the pockets in his combats and produced a twenty pence piece which he handed to Dave.

'Here you go Dave.'

'Good lad. And tell your mates I don't want any trouble tonight will you.'

'Yeah, yeah, good as Gold tonight Dave' said Loz cheekily.

'Yeah alright lad, so it's your last day of school then eh! time to get a job and join the real world now. What's it going to be the Army or Navy?'

'Army or Navy. The one time I think about the Army and Navy is when I'm out shopping Dave.'

Dave understood the joke and laughed.

'Nope, I reckon it's down the dole office first thing Monday morning.'

Dave tutted and waved Loz through. He ambled through a short passage that led to some stairs. He passed some other youths as they walked up the stairs. They nodded to each other. At the bottom of the stairs was a large red wooden door. As Loz opened the door the music hit him. He stepped inside the room to the sound of Terry Hall singing *'Too much too young'*. It was the live version from the single with the photograph of Skinheads on the sleeve. Several youths were dancing in the middle of the dance floor. The dance floor also doubled up as the five a side football pitch and Judo lessons on normal youth club days. The room was narrow. Approximately thirty feet long with a low ceiling. Above head height there were narrow windows covered in a mesh wire. The windows looked out into the alley way where Loz had been greeted by the older Mods a few moments earlier. Loz spotted Den and his friends in one area of the room. There group had swelled to around twenty in total, they were all older, stylish Mods of both genders.

At the far end of the room was a table with the record player placed on it and a few disco lights. There were several boxes of records and carry bags on the floor beside the table. A bunch of girls crowded in one of the corners of the room. They looked like Duran Duran groupies and Madonna clones. Through the swirling disco lights Loz spotted a girl he knew called Theresa. She stood on the fringes of the Duran Duran groupies with her friend Steph. Theresa caught Loz staring at her and smiled. As Loz reciprocated the smile he felt a tap on his shoulder.

'Alright Loz. Nice cycling shirt,' said Robert.

'Cheers, and that's a new shirt aint it?'

'Yep.' Robert replied fiddling with the shirts button on the back of the collar.' It was a finishing school present from my mum.'

'Ditto.'

'The others are upstairs. You coming?'

Loz nodded, took another glimpse at Theresa and followed Robert out through the wooden doors and back up the stairs. Dave was still lingering by the entrance collecting his 20p's. Robert led the way into a large room which was the main hub of the youth club. To the right of the room was a juke box and to the left a pool table. Behind the pool table was the tuck shop. A few more Madonna clones were topping themselves up on chewy sweets. Between the tuck shop and pool table was a beaten up old sofa with a few more beaten up old arm chairs around it. Robert and Loz noticed their friends sprawled out on the sofa and walked over to them.

'Here he is then' said Gregg sarcastically. Gregg was a thick set youth wearing a white jumper. He sported the beginnings of a moustache.

'Oh yeah! Here we thought you were getting here early,' added another young man wearing the same jumper only it was the tank top version.

'It is early' answered Loz.

'You just wanted more time to make sure you look your best for Theresa didn't you?' Steve teased. He looked like he had not been home yet since burning his school blazer earlier at school.

'Bollocks,' replied Loz regretting his curt response suspecting it may add more fuel to the fire. And it did.

16

'Hope you remembered to give your helmet a scrub Loz,' cried Piggy who was the largest boy in Loz's gang. Loz screwed his nose up in Piggy's direction. Piggy mirrored the same back with the addition of mouth full of sweets. Loz squeezed in between a couple of his friends on the sofa and Robert perched himself on the arm of it.

'Did you get an eye full of Theresa and Steph down stairs?' asked Robert taking a sip from someone's bottle of fizz that had been left on the table.

'No. Were they down there then?'

'Yeah. That Steph arrived just as I did. I tell you what I'm gonna have a crack at her later. How about you? You gonna have a crack at Theresa tonight. She likes you.'

'So I've heard' said Loz trying to sound aloof 'Anyway I dunno mate. But you crack on and sort yourself out.'

'You may as well Loz. The rumour is that she does blow jobs.'

Loz frowned at his friend before they were both distracted by the sound of the music coming up from the room below them. The Skat, skat, skat sound of Ska had been replaced by the smoother sounds of Northern Soul.

'Come on' urged Loz deciding this was their cue to head off back down stairs. The other boys sitting around the sofa agreed and set off in the direction of the disco below. Within a few minutes they had joined in with the dancing on the crowded dance floor. The older Mods danced nearest to the DJ whilst the younger ones filled the rest of the room. Everybody demonstrated their best Northern Soul side to side shuffles. A couple of the older Mods attempted some spins and back drops to varying degrees of success. 'There's a ghost in my house' started to play and the dance floor erupted into vigorous dancing. Loz instantly reacted to one of his favourite Northern Soul tunes. He changed gear and slid from side to side with added conviction. He praised himself on his choice of foot wear. For some unknown reason he felt he always glided with more ease in his boxing boots. Someone brushed up against Loz and he turned to see who it was. Den was grinning like a Cheshire cat and gave Loz a thumb's up. Loz suddenly felt ten feet tall realizing that some of his friends had seen the gesture from Den.

Loz was in the zone and stayed on the dance floor for the next three songs, 'Tainted Love', 'What' and 'The Snake'. They were three stormers and stompers in Loz's opinion. Plus they were three records that graced his personal record collection. By the time 'The Snake' faded Loz's cycling shirt was drenched in sweat and clung to his skin. It was not a sensation that Loz enjoyed. He stepped away from the dance floor and found a dark space to cool down. From here he viewed the spectacle of his friends dancing. Piggy wobbled on the spot. Steve shuffled out of time with the music and Robert tried his best to slide gracefully across the dance floor. Loz noticed Steph watching Robert and suspected that Robert had realized. Just as Loz caught his breath and was tempted to re-join the dancing he felt a tap on his arm. He turned to see Theresa dangling a bottle of coke in front of him.

'Wanna sip?' she asked.

Loz was surprised to see her and searched for something suitable to say. He kicked himself as he heard the words 'No I think I'm alright' stumble from out of his mouth.

'Oh, ok,' replied Theresa disappointedly. She looked dejected and turned away as if to walk off. Loz acted swiftly and grabbed her by the arm.

'Mmm, actually, yeah, I'm gasping,' he blurted out and took the coke bottle from her. He took a large sip and winced. The coke was laced with Vodka. Theresa laughed dramatically as she took the bottle from him. Loz watched her take a swig from the bottle. She was a pretty girl and of a similar age and height to Loz. They had both attended schools that shared the same name. One school for boys only, the other for girls and kept separate by all means possible. She had peroxide bleached blonde hair which was cut to a shoulder length. The side of her hair was brushed upwards and held in place with a great deal of hair spray. She had a similar appearance to the blonde girl in The Human League.

Theresa had a mature edge to her that even exceeded most of her friends. She had also developed tits far earlier than her friends. This was a point that Loz and his friends had noticed several months earlier. It was as if one day her tits just appeared out of thin air. It was around that time that Loz became aware that he felt an attraction to her. Before then they didn't have anything to do with each other. The attraction that Loz felt towards Theresa had been observed by his friends. This had feed the rumour that Loz and Theresa would be 'getting off' with each other at the disco.

As Loz stood next to Theresa he realized that he felt a mixture of excitement and nerves. He hoped that she felt the same. He scrutinised her trying to detect a hint of nervousness. When he could not detect anything he was left feeling even more nervous. He felt his mouth drying up and asked for another swig of her concoction.

'I heard you set fire to your school tie.' Theresa asked.

'Yep, and my school blazer' he bragged, then continued 'Loads of us did it. It was really funny. Did you do anything to your uniform?'

'No way! I'm going to keep my uniform so I can show it to my kids.' She looked both serious and cute.

Loz suddenly felt immature in her presence and a little foolish. The introduction of Dave and Ansel Collins 'Monkey Man' was a much needed distraction. It also heralded another Ska set. The dancers on the floor adjusted their moves to fit in with the skanking rhythm. Loz noticed that Theresa appeared unimpressed with the change in music and asked.

'Don't you like Ska?'

Theresa screwed up her cute button nose.

'Come on then, let's go back up stairs,' Loz suggested and she nodded.

Loz led the way conscious that Theresa would be checking him out as she followed. The main room was much busier than before. Somebody had turned the juke box on and Blondie was singing *'Call me'*. A few teenagers played pool whilst others either sat or stood the around the room conversing.

'There's nowhere to sit' noted Loz.

'Hmm. Let's try the T.V room' suggested Theresa and led the way.

The T.V room was small with a large television and another beaten up sofa. There were also several bean bags scattered over the floor. There were no other young people in the room. Loz suddenly felt nervous again.

'Let's see what's on the box shall we?' said Theresa and turned the knob on the television. The familiar music from *Coronation Street* was in full flow. Theresa gestured for Loz to take a seat on the sofa. She then turned off the 'big' light switch. Loz felt his heart skip a beat as Theresa plonked herself down on the sofa close to him.

'Does your mum watch this?' asked Loz trying to evade his nervousness.

'Yea, of course. My mum watches all of them. *Dallas, Crossroads, Dynasty*. I like them too.'

'Right' said Loz.

They sat in silence for a few minutes, both pretending to watch *Coronation Street*. Loz liked the sensation of Theresa sitting so close to him. There thighs touched gently. Slowly and cautiously Loz lifted his arm and placed it around Theresa's shoulder. She said nothing nor resisted. A few more minutes passed where they both sat in silence. Loz stared blankly at the TV but did not see it. He was mapping out his next move in his mind. The familiar 'Corrie' trumpet sounded again indicating a commercial break. The raise in volume spoilt the mood and Loz lost his train of thought. Not that it mattered. Theresa leaned over and planted a moist kiss onto his dry lips. She placed one of her palms onto his cheek and looked adoringly at him. Loz kissed her back and embraced her. Their kissing became increasingly passionate and Loz felt the bulge in his pants grow. He felt his hard cock pushing against the inside of his combat trousers. He hoped Theresa would not notice his erect cock pleading to be let out of its cage.

Their tongues embraced each other's. Loz noted that Theresa's breath tasted of vodka and Mint chewing gum. Then feeling bold Loz casually slipped his hand up inside of her sweat shirt that had 'Choose Life' printed on it. Theresa released a small sensual sigh. Loz groaned in response. It was his attempt at joining in with the noise making. He slid his hand up until it rested on her breast. The cup size must have been slightly too big because Loz easily pushed his fingers under the bra. He fondled her erect nipple. He felt the bulge in his pants get even bigger and harder. He had to shuffle a bit to feel more comfortable. Their bodies got hotter and sweatier. As Loz swopped breast's Theresa pushed her hand down inside of Loz's combats and into his pants. It felt good. Loz groaned again and Theresa moaned.

Their kissing became more passionate as they explored each other's bodies. Theresa bit Loz's bottom lip and he yelped.

'Ssshhh,' she whispered and gripped his cock harder.

19

Loz removed his hand from her breasts and lowered it to her thigh area where he pulled up her 'Ra Ra' skirt. Theresa wriggled herself into a more accommodating position. Loz got excited by her eagerness. Theresa eased her legs apart and Loz accepted the invitation.

Then just as she started to rub his cock faster the T.V room door swung open. A young tubby boy burst into the room and then jumped at the sight before him. He dropped a handful of his crisps onto the floor.

'Err, sorry,' the boy mumbled with his mouth full.

'Just fuck off will you,' Loz shouted.

The boy turned and scampered off ignoring to close the door behind him. The sounds of The Jam's 'Going Underground' were being played on the juke box. It had been on the juke box for the past two years along with 'Start'. Theresa giggled and removed Loz's hand. She looked down at his erect cock pushing against the inside of his combats. To save him the embarrassment of having to stand up and close the door she did it. Loz sorted himself out and wiped the sweat from his forehead with his shift sleeve. Theresa strolled back over to him. He held out his arms to embrace her. Instead of falling into his arms she fell onto her knees in front of him. Theresa had a cheeky sparkle in her eye.

Loz looked down at her nervously. Loz sighed with relief after her performance. It was the best feeling he had ever experienced. Theresa knew exactly what she was doing. Loz decided this was not her first time. The rumours are true he saluted. He watched her mouth work its wonders on him in between catching glimpses of Vera Duckworth on the screen. He heard her mutter something and then it happened. He groaned and she gurgled. At that moment he felt he grew up a few inches.

HEADSTART FOR HAPPINESS

Following his bowl of cereal and a slice of toast Loz had slipped on his deck shoes and set off towards town to meet Robert. The warm sunny day hinted at opportunities and possibilities. It was the first Saturday of the school holidays. The day that announced the holidays had officially begun. It was still only ten o'clock. Loz was not one to sleep in. He had too much youthful energy to burn. The excitement from the previous night put a bounce in his step. He felt like he was gliding down the street. He passed the 'Home Brew' shop and the hairdressers and crossed the road. To his right was an old grey stone wall that had been the original wall to the St Paul's church. The church had burnt down several years before Loz had been born. The only picture he had ever seen of the church was only with his mum and dad on the steps of the church as they were leaving it, having just been married. To his left was an even bigger old Grey stone wall. This was the outer wall to the prison. The prison had been made famous for two reasons. One of the Kray's spent some time incarcerated within it and the large wooden gates were the ones used in the nineteen seventies television series called Porridge.

Loz chose to walk on the sunny side of the road out of the shadow of the giant prison wall. As he walked he could hear the prisoners inside laughing and cheering. He presumed they were playing football rather than rioting. The sun warmed his face as he strained to remember details from his first blow job. He chuckled out loud as he recalled some of Theresa's last mutterings 'Whatever you do, DON'T come in my mouth'.

At the bottom of the road he turned left, still following the walls of the prison. There was a pub called the Hare. The pub had been blown up by an IRA bomb in the mid Seventies. The location of the pub meant that it was frequented by the local squaddies. There was an army barracks less than a mile away. The IRA had obviously targeted the soldiers but to Loz's memory nobody had actually been killed in the blast. However Loz's dad had been walking home from his work in the nearby Royal Mail sorting office. He had only been three hundred feet away when the bomb exploded. He escaped uninjured. In time the pub was rebuilt and refurbished and the squaddies moved onto another nearby pub for a while.

Fifty feet on from the pub Loz passed the local council offices. He had a soft spot for the area. When Loz was much younger his mum worked in the offices as a cleaner. She got paid every Thursday. So each Thursday Loz and his sister and brother was allowed to race down the meet her after she finished her work. Loz's mum would then give each of them a few pence to buy some sweets with on the way home from one of the corner shops. Loz retained fond memories of those Thursdays. Only years later did he realize that it was a nice and generous gesture from his mum. His family were not poor but they were certainly not rich. Everything happened in moderation. They were only ever allowed two biscuits from the tin at any one time. Loz knew both his mum and dad had made sacrifices for their children. He hoped that one day he would be able to repay their kindness and generosity.

A few minutes later Loz passed the first shops that indicated that he had joined the town. A few paces more and he caught sight of Robert standing with another of their friends named Neil. Robert saw Loz and waved. The two boys stood outside a menswear shop called 'Hucks'. Neil was dressed in a purple and black boating blazer, white shirt and blue jeans. The look complete with his recently purchased black and blue bowling shoes from a shop in Carnaby Street. Robert wore his familiar uniform of a polo shirt, jeans and loafers. As Loz got nearer to them they started clapping and chanting 'Gobble, gobble, gobble'. Loz cringed at first then felt a sense of pride as they continued to congratulate him. However to disguise his feelings he greeted them with.

'Oi fuck off. How did you hear about it anyway?'

Loz was curious to know how they knew about his victory. He had not mentioned anything and he couldn't believe that Theresa would mouth off. Robert and Neil continued to milk the situation until Robert revealed how they had heard.

'Word spreads fast mate. Some little tubby kid from the youth club saw you. I think he is Maggie's younger brother.'

'Bollocks. He didn't see anything. He only walked into the TV room when she was giving me a hand job' remarked a confused Loz.

'That's what you think. It turns out he was peeping through one of them small narrow windows from the alley way' laughed Robert.

Loz kicked himself. He had overlooked the windows. Suddenly Loz was overcome with a horrible sense of dread and anxiety. What if Theresa hears the 'gobble gobble' teasing? She will assume he had been responsible and been bragging to everyone. Loz liked Theresa and he did not want to do anything to upset her. Robert noticed Loz stroking his chin as if deep in concentration.

'Don't worry Loz the truth will out. Besides I'm sure she has already told all her mates you have only got a small cock.'

'Funny boy!' Loz barked.

'Look' said Robert pointing at the 'Hucks' shop window 'I like that dog tooth suit'.

The three boys stepped nearer to the window. The shop displayed a collection of Boating blazers and buttoned down shirts. Dotted around the display was a selection of tee shirts with pictures of bands on them like The Jam, The Beat, and The Clash. The floor was covered in loafers and brogues, a mixture of Jam shoes, 'Stage' and 'Cycling'. Plus several Army boots, Monkey Boots and Desert boots. Loz and his friends had spent several years buying their clothes from the shop. In their town 'Hucks' was the only place to buy the clothes their fashion dictated. The shop also catered for the needs of Rude Boys, Skinheads and Punks. It was also the place where Loz's school uniform had been purchased in his later years. These were black sta-prest trousers and white button down shirts. Footwear wise Loz had gotten away with black brogues or loafers. The three boy's ogled at the items they wish they had but could not afford. Robert marvelled at the tank top jumpers. Neil had his eye on the Union Jack blazer but Loz's gaze had fallen on a single lonely mannequin bolted on the end of the windows display.

'What the fuck is that all about?' roared Robert noticing what Loz was staring at.

The mannequin adorned a look that appeared out of place alongside the other garments. It displayed a maroon, grey and white Argyle pattern V-neck jumper with an emblem of a lion over the left breast. Then there were pale blue faded jeans with an image of a bull on the badge on the rear pocket. At the base of the mannequin lay a pair of white trainers with a blue tick shape on the side. The three boys looked at the clothes suspiciously. They stood in silence processing a mixture of fascination and curiosity. Neil looked disgusted, Robert looked intrigued but Loz was captivated.

'I've seen pictures of this stuff in the newspapers' began Neil 'It's what they call football casuals. It's the new look in London and every other footy town. The northerners claim that they started it off but that's bound to be bollocks'.

'The Northerners'. They haven't produced anything since the Wigan Casino. Nay, that's not a look that's going to catch on' proclaimed Robert.

'It looks like the clobber my dad's mate's wear when they go to golf' laughed Neil.

'Yea, and Ronnie Corbett,' added Robert.

'I quite like it' announced Loz still looking and absorbing the sight.

'Bollocks to that Loz,' said Neil.

'No, I do. There's something fresh about it.'

Robert and Neil looked at the mannequin again but screwed their noses up at it.

'I mean, for fucks sake. We have been dressing like Mods since we were eleven years old. Can you honestly say that you're not a little bored with dressing the same all the time?'

Robert and Neil looked at each other and then at Loz shaking their heads in disgust.

'Na once a mod always a mod,' replied Neil as he walked away from the shop. Robert followed. Loz studied the mannequin again and tried to imagine himself dressed like it. The image formed easily.

'You coming then?' yelled Robert who had already started to walk off in the direction of town.

Loz nodded and caught them up. The town was already busy with shoppers bustling about. As usual, Loz recognized several faces. It was one of the things that he liked about growing up in one town. There was a sense that everybody knew everybody else. Everything about the town was familiar to Loz. He knew the streets well and he felt that he understood the people he shared the town with. He felt like he belonged. He was in no rush or need to leave the place.

'Let's nip into 'Our Price'' suggested Robert.

Robert led the way and they entered through the record shops doors.

'Shit' said Neil referring to the Big Country song that blared out from the shops speakers. Robert nodded in agreement. Loz did not. He had a soft spot for Big Country. The shops aisles were stacked with album after album. All categorised in alphabetical order starting with the A's at the entrance to the shop, Abba to Bowie to Culture Club to Duran Duran and so on. The three boys knew where to look and headed for a section tucked away in the far corner of the shop. The label advertised Northern Soul. The three crowded around and flicked through the albums.

'Got it, got it, haven't got that, got It,' murmured Neil.

'Ah, *For Dancers Only*,' that reminds me I loaned my copy out and must get it back' commented Robert.

Loz glanced around the shop. Several bread heads were dribbling over one of the Led Zeppelin albums and chatting adoringly about Jimmy Pages guitar playing. I bet they don't know Page use to play in The Yardbirds Loz thought to himself smugly. The shop keeper had scruffy dyed Black hair and wore a Black tee shirt with Bauhaus advertised on it. He watched a group of girls dressed similar to him except they wore tee shirts of The Cure and wore masses of black mascara. The shop keeper seemed to be admiring the girls torn fish net stockings look. Loz liked the look to. He had always liked it when the Skinhead girls wore torn fish nets. He liked their feather cut hair styles too especially on a girl with a trim body. Big Country faded and something by The Cure begun.

'Come on!' said Neil, 'Definitely time to fuck off.'

The others agreed and exited the shop and turned right. Outside was a large store which was on their left where around twenty Mods had gathered. Several of them clutched crash helmets whilst still wearing their Army surplus green fish tail parkas. Others held hands with their ultra-cool looking girlfriends wearing pencil skirts or ski-pants. As Loz and his two friends approached the gathering Loz spotted Den amongst the group. Because he was much taller he towered over the others. He looked sharp in his white denim jacket with a sheriff's badge sparkling on the breast pocket. Den didn't notice Loz join the group.

'Alright' yelled a voice. It was Paul, Neil's older brother. Paul had spent years bouncing between being a Mod or a Skinhead. Because of this he had friends in both camps. Paul was much respected amongst his peers. He was switched on, friendly and tough. Loz liked him.

'What's going on?' asked Neil.

Paul leaned forward and whispered.

'A couple of us are going to nip into the store before we head off to the Wander Inn. Do you want to tag along?'

Loz, Robert and Neil nodded gratefully. They knew that any opportunity to be seen with the older Mods would do their individual reputations a world of good. Loz secretly looked around the gathering. From what he could see all the main faces were present. There was Reid, one of the oldest Mods who had seen The Jam dozens of times. Then there was Sarge whose dad was in the Army. Sarge was a recent member to the Mod squad having only lived in the town for a year. He was from Sheffield and hard as nails. Then there was Wolfy and his twin brother Raymond, or Ray if you were part of his 'In crowd'. They claimed they had a cousin in the band Purple Hearts but nobody honestly believed them. The final face was Charlie. Charlie was considered the hardest mod in town. His dad had come from East End London and had been an original mod from the sixties. Charlie often held court retelling stories about his dads Brighton beach pitch battles from nineteen sixty four.

The thing the faces had in common was that they had all been Mods since nineteen seventy eight when the new breed kicked off. They had been fulfilling their promise of their misspent youths to the sound track from The Jam, Secret Affair, Merton Parkas and Purple Hearts to name only a few from that crop of new modernists. They had also earned their spurs via beer, brawling and bowling shoes. Loz was insanely jealous of them for being older and privileged enough to of seen those bands live. Especially the most revered of the group, The Jam. At this time in Loz's life not being born five years earlier was his major regret. If he had he knew he would have gotten to see The Jam. That was another thing the older Mods bragged about. They had attended the final gig The Jam ever played at Wembley. That was a couple of years earlier and they still mourned the loss of their favourite band. Loz mourned with them in secret. The Jam had been his ultimate band. The Jam was the reason Loz was a Mod. The first record he ever bought with his own money was 'That's Entertainment'. It had been his birthday and with fifty pence worth of birthday money Loz had wandered off into town on a mission to purchase the seven inch record. That afternoon he played the record a hundred times and greedily lapped up every second of it.

Apart from Den the other faces rarely gave Loz and his friends the time of day. Den was different. He had always been approachable and accessible. Den had style and a cool presence about him. He didn't have to work at it. Being cool came naturally to him. Loz had first befriended Den via the connection to his sister. One of Dens friends use to be Loz's sister's boyfriend. The said boyfriend and Den occasionally visited Loz's house during that period and whilst the boyfriend stole a few private moments with Loz's sister Den and Loz would sit around drinking tea. The friendship was truly sealed after Den challenged Loz to list every Jam release. Loz did it with ease and his performance had impressed Den.

'Right, I'll be back in a minute,' said Paul and turned to set off in the direction of the store.

'Here hold on, I'm coming' said Neil grabbing hold of his brother sleeve.

Loz and Robert folded their arms and waited for Neil to return.

'There's a new series of *Tuckers Luck* started up. Did you see it?' asked Robert.

'Shit no, I missed it. Has Tucker ditched that leather jacket and those red socks yet?'

'Nope, he still has them. It's good though. Mind you it's got nothing on *Grange Hill*. That was the best when Tucker and the others were in it.'

Loz agreed.

'I wish they would run the *Water Margin* again. It's so much better than *Monkey*. I really like the theme tune. It's brilliant.'

'I prefer *Monkey* actually. But hey each to their own,' replied Robert.

'Here what's that poster' said Loz heading off towards the newsagents shop window. Robert followed Loz. The poster was of Paul Weller with slick back hair. He had a Yellow jumper slung around his neck like some American college boy and had a pink shirt with black and red tie. Weller was holding up a poster of another band called The Questions.

'I suppose Weller is promoting his record label Respond.' Said Robert

'Yeah, I really like the stuff on the label. Well, the bits I've heard. That Tracie is a bit special too' replied Loz.

Loz stood admiring Weller's latest image. He decided it was not that far removed from the football casuals look which adopted the pastel colour jumpers and shirts. Loz was not keen on the oily creamed slick back hair look though. However it did prove the point that Weller was one big massive fucking step in front of everyone else.

'What you up to?' came a familiar voice that startled him.

Loz turned to see his sister who stood glaring at him alongside her four friends, Lisa, Debbie, Sharon and Sam. All four of them wore brightly coloured jump suits and mixed Gold and plastic jewellery together. They all had highlights in their hair. 'Bollocks' thought Loz hoping the older Mods had not noticed his sister and her friends. In his opinion they were embarrassing.

'So?' Loz's sister asked again.

'Nothing much really we are just waiting for Neil to come back from the store.'

Lozs sister glanced at the crowd of Mods who were all laughing at Pig Bin Billy one of the local tramps.

'If mum knew you were hanging around with that lot she would blow her top'.

'Well, she won't know anything unless you say something will she?' spat Loz.

'Just be careful' she replied already walking off with her friends. Loz sighed, he didn't think the older Mods had noticed. Then without warning his sister and her friends turned around and squealed 'Gobble Gobble Gobble'. Instantly the older Mods turned their attention away from Pig Bin Billy and focussed on Loz. Loz felt the blood rush to his face. He felt like he must look like a lonely Red letter box. 'Gobble Gobble Gobble' yelled some of the older Mods.

Fortunately their taunts were cut short as they were alerted to some hustling and bustling near the entrance to the store. Suddenly the group of Mods began to disperse in various directions. Loz realized something was happening. He was also grateful that whatever it was had diverted attention from him. Neil and Paul appeared from the chaotic crowd and grabbed hold of Loz and Robert.

'Come on, leg it,' screamed Paul.

The four of them ran down the street weaving in and out of shoppers. Once they felt they had reached a safe distance from the store they slowed their pace. They adjusted to a casual stroll trying to blend in with the Saturday shoppers. Loz felt the rush of adrenalin ease and caught his breath. He looked questionably at Neil who just grinned back at him. Paul led the way through the market buildings and across the road. They passed the town's prized statue of Queen Victoria and headed off down Bank Street. This part of town was quieter. They followed the street until they came across a row of six scooters parked side by side. A mixture of Vespa and Lambretta with their Chrome panels gleaming and shinning in the sun light. One male sat stretched over his Lambretta TV 175 with a brilliant blue and white paint job. Den smiled at Loz and his friends.

'Alright chaps, you all look a bit flushed,' he observed. Den had not been present when the gathering of Mods had dispersed in a rush. He had left the group several minutes before.

'Ta for playing '*Out on the floor*,' last night' said Loz.

'No probs Loz. You looked like you had a good night. You're a good little dancer too.'

Loz grinned and felt like the 'Ace Face' of the Howard Wardell. Loz and Den exchanged a few more words about the disco then they entered through the doors of the Wander Inn.

Paul led the way and plonked himself down on one of the larger tables near the back of the café. The café was noisy with its coffee machines hissing away. It was also hot due to no air conditioning. The smell of bacon and sausages cooking was inviting and made them all feel hungry. There was already a young male sat at the table. Baz knew Loz well. He had been involved in an up and down relationship with his sister for a couple of years. Baz was of slight build. He had neatly cut had brown hair and bushy eye brows. Half of his family were Italian and the other half Bermondsey. He had a darkish Mediterranean like complexion. Baz was resting his arm on his open face crash helmet. He wore a red and yellow thick candy stripe shirt. The shirt was made of Italian cotton of course. Loz slid along the seat so he sat opposite Baz who sipped at his luke warm tea. Baz raised his bushy eyebrows.

The waitress appeared holding her note book and glanced around the boys waiting to take their orders. They ordered two pots of tea and shuffled in their seats. Neil and Paul riffled around in their jackets and begun to remove tape cassettes. Loz tutted, realizing what all the commotion back at the store had been to do with. He gaped at the two brothers as they built a pile of cassettes on the table.

'Fucking hell,' gasped Robert 'did you leave anything in the shop.'

'Yea, all of Elton John's stuff,' laughed Paul.

27

The table was soon covered in a scattering of cassettes as the others on the table helped themselves to the stolen tapes. There were albums from Madness, Faith Brothers, Jo Boxers and the brilliant Dexy's Midnight Runners album *'Searching for the young soul rebels'*. Loz snatched the Dexy's up. He only had a copy of the album on vinyl. Loz wiped some sauce stains off the tape and asked if he could have it. Neil nodded. Loz looked around at his group of friends. He felt proud of them. They were just average Saturday's kids who lived in council and terraced houses. They had no unrealistic aspirations. Notions of university were alien to them. They were rough and ready and enjoying themselves. Loz doubted that any of them would regret their childhoods. He smiled inside.

'Not a bad stash,' commented Den who had now joined them at their table.

Loz slipped the tape inside his jacket pocket feeling a little ashamed.

'Anything left for me?' Den added searching through the leftovers on the table. He held a Bad Manners album between his thumb and forefinger, thought for a few moments then put it down. He ordered a cup of tea. The group sat and discussed the raid on the store and how easy it was to steal from them. It was not Neil's and Pauls first time. The group chatted and sipped at their teas until Baz glared out of the window and said 'Oh shit'. The others turned abruptly to see what Baz had spotted. A dark Green Cortina pulled up alongside Dens scooter that was parked up outside. Whilst they had been busy exploring the stolen cassettes they had not heard the 'pop pop' sound of the other scooters ride off.

The Cortina's doors flung open and four Skinheads climbed out. Loz and his friends instantly recognised them. They were four of the hardest Skinheads in town with fearsome reputations. The tallest of the Skinheads name was Webby. He was the leader of their gang. He was similar age to Den and his arch enemy. Webby's gang consisted of Walshy who was the fattest member with a tattoo of a spiders web over one side of his neck, Roy was the wildest member and had a scissor incision tattooed around his throat and Simmons who had a ACAB tattoo which stood for 'All Cops Are Bastards' tattooed onto his knuckles. But Webby was a notch above the rest who took pleasure in executing his menacing imaginative creations onto his victims. He especially liked his victims to be Mods. Webby had a single tattoo which was a tear that hung from the side of one of his eyes. All four Skinheads had one tattoo in common. They had the West Ham United football club badge tattooed onto their left forearms.

The four skins were dressed top to toe in button down shirts, braces, jeans which were shortened to reveal their Ox blood army boots with white laces. All sported a cropped grade one severe haircut. Loz senses the nervousness at their table. Only Den appeared to remain calm and confident. Loz and his friends stared out of the window watching Webby snarling and verbally assaulting Dens scooter. The other skinheads stood around and appeared to be joining in with the abuse. Den rose up from his seat and stood tall and proud with his arms folded. Loz wondered what he was intending to do. Loz prayed that he Skinheads would exhaust their abusing of the scooter and move on to find some other poor victims. Loz did not care who they may be just as long as it was not him and his friends. But the Skinheads seemed to be enjoying themselves too much. Simmons leapt on to Dens scooter and started to play around with the gears. Den could stand it no more. He needed to protect his scooter and his pride. Den headed for the door and walked out of the café. Loz and his group watched intently as Den walked straight up to Simmons and shout something an inch away from his face. Simmons reacted aggressively and pushed Den away. Den regained his balance but not before Roy landed a punch onto the side of Den's jaw. Den stumbled and rocked slightly then reciprocated a punch.

'We can't stay here,' cried Loz.

The others just looked blankly back at him. Then Paul jumped up and encouraged the rest of them to follow him. Paul led the way closely followed by Loz, then the others. They piled out of the café just as Den was absorbing kicks and punches from the Skins. Loz launched the first attack and struck a punch onto one of the unsuspecting Skinhead's nose. Loz heard the sound of bone cracking and blood spurted out. Paul and Neil dragged another of the Skinheads away from Den and released a volley of punches into his body. Baz and Robert chose Walshy, the fat Skin to unleash their anger onto. Walshy spat abuse at them as he tried to avoid their punches. From out of the corner of Loz's eye he could see Den and Webby going at it. The six Mods fought courageously against the four Skinheads for several minutes until all ran out of energy. One after the other the two groups separated and the Skins retreated to their car. They jumped inside puffing and panting and hurled abuse and threats at their opponents as they drove away. Loz dropped to the pavement. The abuse did not bother him but the threats did. Den collapsed on the floor next to Loz and started to laugh. Loz could only manage a wry smile. His cheek bones and stomach ached. Then one by one the others plonked themselves so that they also sat perched on the edge of the pavement. They caught their breath and launched into recounting the event to each other. Each informed the other how they had thrown kicks and punches at their opponents. They were still congratulating each other on their apparent victory when a bunch of the older Mods rode up to the café on their scooters.

They parked their scooters, removed their helmets and marvelled at the sight of Den and his companions. It was evident they had all been involved in some kind of fracas. Loz and his friends felt ten feet tall as Den explained what had occurred to the older Mods. Sarge and Reid appeared especially impressed. This fight had scored Loz and his friends many brownie points. The adoration outweighed their bruises. The group eventually took their conversation and back patting back inside of the Wander inn. They drank more tea and treated themselves to bacon sandwiches. Loz sat between Den and Reid feeling the dog's bollocks.

A few days ate into the school holidays and Loz continued to feel the high from the fight and his first blow job. He bathed in the thought that he had cemented a few large blocks into his wall of reputation. Life was feeling good he told himself as he lay flat out on his bed wearing only his boxing shorts. Playing at low volume was The Style Councils 'Café Bleu' album. The album had taken a while to grow on Loz and most of his friends. Weller's most recent creative injection challenged many of his loyal supporters. The Jam was a different band who reflected a different time. The new Jazzier vibe that Weller was connecting to was not every Jam fans cup of tea. Loz was the same at first but slowly the album was drip fed into his soul. Loz admired Paul Weller's instinct for modernism. Through Weller Loz was reminded that the whole point of the modernist was to move on. The motivation for the original Mods was to be different and to explore and discover new areas. Weller was on the cutting edge of this and expressed himself through his music. It's exactly what Weller had done with The Jam at a time when the majority of kids were still sucking the tit of mother punk. Loz owed his infatuation with Mod to Weller and The Jam. They had introduced him to the original bands from the sixties like The Small Faces, Who, Creation. Loz would know he would always be eternally grateful for this.

Loz sighed as he reminded himself of the mannequin dressed in the casual clobber in the 'Hucks' shop window. Was this the next step for the modernist he mused? He felt that he would need to investigate further. Something inside of him told him that change was afoot. He sensed that something was in the air. Something new and fresh was calling him. Loz felt a twang of excitement. He sensed that he was changing. In a just a few days he had left school for good and experienced his first blow job. The older Mods even knew his name now and that was a bonus too.

'Café Bleu' continued to play. Since Loz had owned the album he had found himself being turned on to Jazz. Jazz was not a music he was familiar with. He did not know any one that owned jazz records but gradually he had picked up some Art Blakey and Buddy Rich albums from boot fairs. For some unknown reason he found himself attracted to the Jazz drumming greats. As a result of having his attention drawn towards the drummers Loz found his attention focusing more and more on Weller's drummer, the young Steve White. Loz liked the fact that Steve White was not that much older than himself. Loz discovered that White lived fairly near to him too, just a few miles away up the M20.

The track 'Me ship came in' began to play. Loz admired Whites use of the rim shot on the track. It was exactly what the song needed he told himself. The song reflected Loz's mood perfectly and he stretched down to pick up his sketch pad from the floor. He flicked through the pages of sketches and drawings until he found the latest piece he had been working on. Loz studied the drawing of the 'Ever changing moods' single cover that he had been copying. The original photograph on the single sleeve was atmospheric and moody. It showed Weller sitting within a cloud of cigarette smoke and wearing a woollen skull cap. The photograph was built on shadows and shading and Loz absorbed himself in the sketching of it. Loz found a pencil and continued to add shading to his drawing. The drawing relaxed him and this was enhanced as the track the 'Paris match' began. The honey tones of Tracy Thorns singing soothed him. He felt content. Loz absorbed himself in the drawing and before long it was complete. As he laid the pad and pencil on the floor 'Dropping bombs on the White House' burst into life. Loz snatched the pencil back up and found another one so that he could drum along to the song. Steve White launched into his drum solo and Loz did his best to keep up with him tapping the pencils furiously onto his knees. The solo built and built until Loz's favourite bit kicked in '1,2, 1,2,3,4' cried Steve White inviting the rest of the band to re-join him. Even Loz was breathing heavily by this stage.

Satisfied that he had unleashed a brilliant drum solo of his own, Loz flung the pencils into the air and leapt up. The Style Council had informed his choice of clothing. Loz searched through his wardrobe for his blue polo shirt and blue jeans that he always kept a one inch turn up on. Next he pulled on a clean pair of white flannel socks and pushed his feet into his favourite tasselled loafers. As he exited his bedroom he grabbed his three quarter length beige trench coat. The one of a similar style to what Weller wore on the 'Café Bleu' album cover.

Loz left an empty house. As he stepped out of the front door and skipped over the two steps that led onto the street he noticed his dad walking up it. His dad was strolling casually with his brown post office bag slung over his shoulder. There must have been no overtime Loz thought to himself. His dad normally worked a shift until eight o clock in the evening after having started at five in the morning. Loz waved at his dad and his dad waved back. Loz then turned left and set off up the street.

TASTE OF PINK

'Alright!' said Robert, opening the front door of his red brick Victorian terrace house. 'Alright!' replied Loz as he invited himself in and entered the hall way.

Robert ushered Loz up to his bed room which was on the second floor. The room smelt musty and screamed teenage boy. A few random pairs of white socks lay scattered around the room and a few tee shirts lay in a heap at the bottom of his bed. On entering the room Loz noticed the grubby old sock that Robert kept under his bed. That sock was always there. Loz never understood why.

Roberts's room was a shrine to everything Two Tone. The entire room was based on the black and white colour scheme. Most of the furniture had been painted either black or white by Robert and some had the dogtooth pattern painted on them. The only splash of colour in the bed room was the Union Jack pattern bed sheet and his discarded tee shirts. The white wallpaper was plastered with countless posters of Roberts's favourite bands. He had glossy posters of all shapes and sizes of The Specials, The Selector, The Beat and The Body Snatchers. Also mixed amongst them were small posters of Prince Buster and other Jamaican artists from the sixties pinned to the wall with drawing pins. It was an impressive display and a homage to Ska music.

Loz perched himself on the edge of Roberts un-made bed and tapped his finger along to the beat of the Upsetters song 'Live injection' that was just coming to an end. Loz picked up the 'Tighten up Volume two ' album cover. Loz admired the breasts and mid riff area of the girl on the sleeve of the album cover as he had done many times before. He owned the 'Tighten up' volumes one and two and had often fantasised over the mysterious black female on the front cover.

'Stunning isn't she' said Robert noticing that Loz was dribbling over the album cover.

'Choice mate. Choice.'

'I wonder what it's like.'

'What?' asked Loz.

'Well, you know, a coloured girl,' said Robert cautiously.

'The same as any other I suppose you plum' answered Loz knowing full well that he had asked himself the same question many times. 'Right' said Robert and continued getting dressed. Loz placed the album cover on the floor besides Robert's old record player and picked up the Richard Barnes book 'Mods'. He flicked through the pages. Loz never tired of looking at the photographs of the original Mods. The book had been his bible for several years. Loz often pondered what it must have been like to of been a teenager in the mid-sixties. He assumed it must have been amazing to ride to Brighton on a scooter and participated in the beach battles with the rockers.

Loz preferred the original sixties mod look better than the look he had grown up. The sixties Mods appeared to have more style and flare dressed in their tailored made suits. Loz liked the idea of being a mod in sixties London. The thought of frequenting the mod clubs of the day like The Flamingo or The Scene thrilled him. Then to actually go and see the mod bands of the era like The Small Faces, The Action or The Creation would have been amazing. Loz continued to flick through the pages of the Mod book until Robert announced he was ready.

'One of your blakeys has fallen off' observed Loz.

'Yeah I know. I'll get my dad to sort it out later' he replied.

They exited the bedroom and headed off down stairs to the kitchen. Robert made a bee line for the biscuit tin and removed the lid. He held the tin out to Loz who dived into the tin and removed two biscuits.

'Have another' invited Robert.

'No it's alright. I'm used to having two. We have a two biscuits rule in our house so I'm used to it.'

'What do you mean a two biscuit rule,' asked Robert putting the lid back on the tin and pushing it towards the bread bin.

'In our house we are only allowed to take two biscuits at a time. If we don't they would all be gone in five minutes and then my mum would get the hump. 'So two biscuit's only.'

Robert shrugged his shoulders and added 'That's fair enough I suppose. Come on then.'

They left Roberts home and walked down the street joking and spitting biscuit crumbs at each other. It was another warm sunny day with an expansive blue sky above them. Apart from a few lumps of white dog shit and a couple of younger kids playing on their 'Grifter' bicycles the street was empty.

'Have you bumped into Theresa yet?' asked Robert.

'No not yet. I suppose it's only a matter of time though.'

'You like her though don't you? You should do, I mean she ain't no old boiler is she.'

Loz didn't reply. He didn't want to share his feelings for Theresa yet. He also was still anxious what her response would be to the 'Gobble Gobble' taunts.

'Shall we give Andy a knock?' said Robert pausing outside the last house on the street.

Loz nodded and they both walked up to the front door and rang the doorbell. Nothing so they rang the doorbell again. They waited for a few moments then decided that Andy was not in so turned to leave. Just then they heard the familiar sound of Andy's croaky voice yell out 'Hold on, hold on'. Then the door swung open and Andy stood in the entrance way with his face all flushed.

'Alright' said Robert 'what you up to?'

'Erm, not much really I'm just watching something on the box. Do you want to come in?'

Loz and Robert pushed past him and headed for the front room where they could hear the unusual sounds of females moaning. On entering the front room Robert shouted 'Fucking hell Andy.'

Andy just smiled and invited his guests to sit down.

'Is that...' begun Loz but he didn't finish his sentence. Instead he gawped at the image on the television screen of a pretty young thing sucking the cock of some athletic looking male swimmer.

'Yep' replied Andy proudly.

'What's this film called then?' asked Loz

'Deep throat, it's one of my brother's videos.' Andy informed.

'Where's your mum?' Asked Robert feeling nervous that Andy's mum may enter the room and catch them watching porn videos.

Andy laughed then said that his mum had gone to Margate for the day with his younger sister. Andy assured his friends that they had nothing to worry about. The three of them continued to watch the film. Occasionally they would giggle nervously. Loz thought the film was stupid really as he watched girls swim amongst giant penises that they had apparently sucked off from their victims. However it did remind him of his first blow job so that excited him as he relived the moment.

The cuckoo clock startled the three boys as it struck five times. Robert shuffled under the cushion that he had plonked onto his lap and Loz stood up indicating that it was time to leave and head off to the Howard Wardell youth club. Robert sorted himself out and Andy disappeared up stairs to replace the porn video amongst his brothers growing collection of blue films and boy's magazines. On the way to the youth club Andy asked to be filled in on the fight with the Skinheads at the Wander inn. Loz and Robert recounted the event like a couple of seasoned warriors.

As they entered the street where the youth club was located they stopped at the pub on the corner. This was where their friend Nips lived. His mum and dad owned the pub. Nips was a much liked character. He was always chirpy, confident and full of Mercurial energy. He had brilliant communication skills which Loz presumed was because he had grown up around the pubs older customers. Nips and Loz had formed a band three years earlier. Nips was going to be the next Pete Townsend strumming along on a battered old five string guitar and Loz thought he was destined to be the next Rick Buckler as he had beaten the shit out of Nip's mum's 'Tupperware' containers. They had even written a song which Nip sung in his best Daltrey impersonation. The lyrics were honest, naïve and prophetic;

'Time is not to be forgotten, Time is what we need, Time is told on a clock or a digital watch'.

The band only lasted two rehearsals before they gave up to chase girls instead. Robert stuck his head in the door of the pub and shouted out Nip's name. The pub was closed until seven o clock but Nip's dad was stacking beer glasses behind the bar. He called out for Nip and few moments later Nip bounced out of the pub door wearing his signature look of desert boots, jeans and a White tee shirt.

'Alright lads, I heard about your run in with the boneheads,' he said 'You know you're going to have to watch your backs now don't you.'

Loz and Robert looked at each other. They knew it was true but had been trying to avoid thinking about it. The four friends strolled casually down the street towards the youth club.

'Your old man looked a bit pissed off Nip,' observed Robert.

'Yes he is. Some prick has stolen the table and chairs from the beer garden.'

'Any ideas who would do that?' added Andy.

'No, not around here but if you see them or hear anything let me know yeah.'

They nodded. A few yards further on they entered through the metal gates of the youth club car park. Several Li, PX, TV and GS scooters were lined up alongside each other. They looked brilliant adorned in leopards skin seat cover's, chrome panelling, additional mirrors and tassels hanging from the handle bars. Loz halted to admire them and spotted a rusty pale blue Vespa Sprint that he had not seen before. He was curious whom it belonged to. Loz longed for the day when he could own his own scooter. He was still just a few months away from being old enough to ride. He dreamt of owning a Lambretta Li 125 in blue and white. He preferred the Lambretta shape over the Vespa.

'Oi Oi' a voice called out and Loz looked to see who it was. Den approached Loz with a few of his friends.

'What do you think?' Den asked pointing to the Vespa Sprint.

'Looks brill, I've never seen a scoot with the two separate seats like that either,' replied Loz.

'Yeah, it is a bit unusual. There were not many scooters made like it.'

Loz watched Den polish the hand bar with the sleeve of his jumper. Loz looked forward to the day when he could do the same thing.

'This Saturday we are going over to Ogart's. The Prisoners are playing,' informed Den.

'Right' replied Loz thinking it was unlikely he could get a lift with his dad any way.

'So, if you want to come, you can use that seat,' invited Den

'Fucking hell, really! Yeah cheers. I've not seen The Prisoners yet.'

Den smiled as he put on his crash helmet and clipped the buckle on under his chin. He then jumped onto his scooter and started the engine. The familiar smell of two-stroke and the sound of the exhaust popping filled the air. Den was joined by his friends who also jumped on their scooters and started up their engines. Within moments the Youth club car park roared with the sound from the scooters engines and the air filled with puffs of two-stroke. Loz loved the sound and smell that scooters produced.

'I'll pick you up at seven' Den shouted over the noise of his scooters engine and led the convoy of scooters out of the car park. Loz jealously watched the scooters ride off up the street. Once they were out of sight and he could no longer hear them he walked up the stone steps towards the youth club entrance. As he entered he was buzzing as he thought about Dens offer to go with him to see The Prisoners.

Dave was sat at his desk and held his hand out. Loz dropped his twenty pence into it and winked. He then walked into the room with the pool table and joined his friends. Nip was beating Robert at pool and Andy was chewing on a chewy bar that he had purchased from the tuck shop. Loz was grinning like a Cheshire cat as he searched in his pocket for another twenty pence.

'What you grinning about?' questioned Robert.

'Den has offered to give me a lift on his new Vespa to Ogart's on Saturday. But the best bit is that The Prisoners are playing.'

'Blimey, that's a stroke of luck. How did you manage that?' returned Robert.

Loz simply shrugged his shoulders and inserted the twenty pence into the juke box. He then pressed the buttons that selected his choice of song and 'Start' by The Jam. He was singing along to the record when he heard a voice say 'Hello'. He recognised the voice as his friends Isabel. Isabel was the same age as Loz. She always kept her brown hair short and had kind brown eyes to match. Isabel was easy going and they had known each other for several years. Isabel lived a few hundred yards from the youth club so frequented the club daily. Isabel was the most stylish mod girl that Loz knew. The Mod look suited her. She smiled at Loz dressed in her navy blue ski pants and a polo shirt.

'I heard about the fight' said Isabel.

Loz could not tell whether she was impressed with him or pissed off with him.

'We had no choice.' Replied Loz selecting the next Jam song 'Going Underground'.

'Appropriate choice that one,' she said nodding to the song that Loz had chosen.

'What do you mean?' he asked.

'You're going to have to go underground now to avoid Webby and his mates. They are going to be looking for you, you know that.'

'Yeah I know' Loz sighed.

'And when they do catch up with you they are going to kick your head in'

'Yeah alright, there's no need to spell it out'. Loz hissed back at her.

'So other than that what else have you been up to?' she asked.

'Well, Den is taking me to see The Prisoners this Saturday' Loz announced proudly.

'Cor, nice one,' Isabel looked pleased for Loz 'Is that why he was here earlier? I saw him and his mates ride past my house.'

'Yea, it must have been. He has a new Vespa too and that's what we are riding on Saturday.'

'Brilliant. Good for you Loz, your with the 'In crowd' now.'

Loz grinned and Isabel took a lick of her orange ice lolly. Loz recognised that Isabel was developing into a fine gentle woman. He admired her simplicity and outlook on life. She didn't have a bad bone in her body and would make someone a fine partner one day. Loz and Isabel leant their backs against the juke box. It was warm and vibrated.

'There's another disco downstairs. I think it will be quiet though coz there's not many here tonight.'

'I suppose lots of people have now gone on their family holidays to Butlins of Pontins.' Loz joked.

'Yeah maybe' replied Isabel walking away 'by the way Theresa is down stairs.' She winked and mouthed 'Gobble Gobble Gobble.'

Loz stuck his tongue out and Isabel did the same. Loz had been dreading having to face Theresa but he also wanted to see her again. He hoped she would be friendly towards him and accepted that he had not spread the 'Gobble' rumour. Loz waited for his records to finish and watched his friends play pool. As The Jam faded he plucked up the courage and decided it was time to go and face the music. He pushed his hands into his pockets and swaggered off downstairs.

Isabel was correct, there was only approximately twenty members bopping around to a Wham song. Loz cringed. Loz scanned the room looking for Theresa but he could not see her. He sighed with relief thinking that Isabel must have made a mistake. Then he heard a voice casually say 'Alright prick?'

Loz swung round to see Theresa standing behind him. She had her arms folded and scowled at him as her top slid off her shoulder revealing her bare skin. She still looked attractive though. Loz spat and mumbled a few apologetic words trying to convince her that he had not been responsible for spreading the 'Gobble gobble' rumour. Theresa simply stood firm swopping from arms folded to hands on hips and glared at him. Loz could not ascertain whether he was making progress or not. Eventually he exhausted himself and resigned to accepting whatever punishment Theresa was going to unleash. He braced himself for the assault then Theresa calmly said 'I know'.

Loz relaxed as Theresa informed him that she had discovered that the tubby young boy who had interrupted them in the T.V room had been the culprit. She explained that she had put two and two together without much trouble. She then said that she had enjoyed letting him sweat a little and kissed him gently on the lips. Loz leaned into her and held her tight and stuck his tongue down her throat. Next Theresa grabbed him by the hand and led him towards the girl's toilets. Once inside she ushered Loz into one of the cubicles and began to undress him. They continued to kiss passionately until both of them cuddled each other's naked bodies. They awkwardly ravished the others body in the tight area. Loz pushed Theresa against the door of the cubicle and kissed her neck and shoulder. Theresa groaned and shuddered. Loz felt thrilled and naughty. A few moments later she pushed him away and onto the toilet seat. She then collapsed onto her knees in front of him and pushed his legs apart. A moment later Loz sighed a deep relief and kissed Theresa on the forehead. She wiped her mouth then popped a Wrigley's chewing gum into it.

Within five minutes they had redressed and sneaked out of the girls toilets unnoticed. Theresa held Loz's hand and led him into the disco room. Loz cringed again as Soft Cell's version of *'Tainted Love'* blared out of the speakers. Theresa smiled at Loz and leaned forward to whisper something in his ear.

'Can you get hold of any Johnnies?' she asked

Loz grinned and nodded back at her thinking to himself that if it was the last thing on earth he could do, it would be getting hold of a packet of Johnnies.

THE KIDS ARE ALRIGHT

Loz spent Saturday afternoon around his Nan's house watching Big Daddy and Giant Haystacks wrestling. Between rounds his Nan filled him with crumpets and cups of tea. At around three o clock Loz's Uncle dropped by for his daily cup of tea. His uncle visited his mum every day at the same time. Loz liked to visit his Nan. Her husband, Loz's granddad whom they called Pop had died when Loz was only eight. Loz had fond memories of his 'pop'. Whenever Loz visited his Nan he would recall something of those days with his granddad. In between laughing at Big Daddy's body bounce off of Giant Haystacks Loz remembered the time his granddad announced that he had a present for him. It turned out that his granddad had been saving tokens from his tobacco packet and had collected enough to get him something.

That particular day Loz had walked the fifty paces from his house to his grandparent's house and had been met at the door by his granddad who sneakily dropped a few mint sweets into his pocket out of his Nans vision. His granddad then took Loz into the front room and handed him a brown paper bag. Loz ripped the bag apart and his face lit up as the gift revealed itself. Loz held in his hands an Action man's kit bag. In the bag was a collection of Action man sized cutlery, plates and other tiny accessories that any Action man would need to fulfil his duty. Loz had been thrilled and took great care of the gift for several days afterwards.

Loz took a sip of his tea and reminded himself how fortunate he was to have a kind and generous family. He then finished his crumpet and said his goodbyes to his Nan and Uncle. He left his Nan's house and walked in the direction of his own. Outside the 'Home Brew' shop a gathering of children played 'What's the time Mr Wolf'. Loz chuckled to himself reminding himself that he was one of them children just a few years before. He too played 'What's the time Mr Wolf, Knock down Ginger and Forty Forty' just like those children. Not much changed in his street. The kids played amongst the cars and the same grumpy neighbours continued to be grumpy.

A young Asian boy called Raj was sitting on the curb outside the 'Home Brew' shop. Raj was one of two young boys that lived in the house next to the corner shop and post office at the top of the street. Raj and his brother Nami were the only remaining Pakistanis at Loz's old school. At one time there had been a third but he had disappeared after the second year. Throughout Loz's five years at his secondary school there only ever been three Asians, two Chinese boys and two coloured boys as they were termed.

Loz greeted Raj and sat down on the curb beside him. The two had become firm friends following an incident that had occurred the year before. One night the street had been abruptly woken up by the sound of glass breaking followed by a volley of shouting and screaming. Loz had jumped out of bed and raced to the front door like many of his neighbours. He stood on the step alongside his mum and dad trying to understand what all the commotion was about. Word spread from neighbour to neighbour like an invisible grapevine. They were informed that a gang of Skinheads had attacked the Patel's post office and home. The Skinheads had hurtled stones at the shop and home windows smashing several of them. Plus to leave their mark they had spray painted the letters 'NF' on the Patel's front door.

The day after his attack Loz had walked to school with Raj. Loz tried to discuss the impact of the previous night's attack but Raj said very little. He appeared to accept that this was how his life was living in England in nineteen eighty four. Loz felt angry on behalf of Raj and his family. He tried to understand what Raj's life must be like to be one of the minorities in the street, the school and the town. Loz admired Raj's courage and tried to convey this to him but he seemed dismissive.

Various rumours abounded as to who the attackers were. However everyone suspected it could only have been Webby and his skinhead gang. The Police never got involved and soon it was old news. The same skinheads returned a few weeks later and repeated the attack. This time no one really batted an eyelid.

'Alright Raj. How's things?' asked Loz.

'Ok, I suppose. My brother and I are going to stay with an Uncle in Bradford for the rest of the summer holidays.'

'That's alright isn't it? Besides you get a decent curry up there eh!'

The two boys laughed then Raj got up, said he needed to go and would catch up when he returned. Loz waved him off and climbed to his feet too. The kids behind him were still playing 'Forty Forty'. It pleased him to see the local kids playing with such freedom. He hoped children would always be safe to serve their youthful apprenticeships on their streets. Loz watched a lone child sitting on the steps of the 'Home Brew' shop playing with a few toy soldiers.

A memory flashed into Loz's mind. He remembered the time when he and his next door neighbour Pete sat on the same steps also playing with small plastic soldiers. They had been joined by one of the younger kids who lived down their street. This child had a bag of tiny metal soldiers dressed and painted ready for the battle of Waterloo. What then unfolded was a scam whereby Loz and Pete distracted the poor child so that they could steal from his bag of soldiers. The younger boy had no idea and after several minutes left with his lighter collection of soldiers.

Loz and Pete compared and shared their stash with each other until they were rudely interrupted by an older girl than them who lived directly opposite the 'Home Brew' shop. It turned out that the girl had watched the whole scam from behind her sash window and now decided to confront the two young thieves. Loz recalled how he and Pete were cornered, threatened and left feeling ashamed. They also returned the soldiers before running home to weep in private.

Loz's trip down memory lane was disturbed as the familiar music of the ice cream van entered the street. The sound of the ice cream alerted all the children playing and they all scattered in different directions in search of their parents and few pence to buy a lolly. Loz chuckled to himself then walked the few steps to his home and descended the steps to the basement. He tried the door and it was open. That meant somebody was home.

Loz entered a dark, dingy, damp smelling room that had a large dining table in the centre. His family occasionally used it to eat their Sunday roast's on. There was one arm chair and a tatty sofa. The arm chair had been in the same spot for years and was a favourite resting place for the various cats over the years. A particular favourite of the family was a cat named Lucy. She was remembered for once giving birth to her litter on the chair. Loz and his sister had watched the event. Loz was left feeling humbled after the experience.

Perhaps Lucy was too.

Loz strolled through the room and entered the kitchen. His Sister was sitting at the table reading a copy of *Jackie*. Neither party acknowledged one another. Loz casually gathered the ingredients for a toasted cheese sarnie and prepared one. He boiled the kettle and made himself a cup of tea. When he opened the fridge to get the milk his eyes lit up. On one of the shelves was a large sponge cake filled with cream and jam. The family called them flying saucers because of their size and shape. He thought about cutting off a slice now but turned to look at his sister. She understood and glared at him. Instead he just took the milk and avoided thinking about the flying saucer. Once the sarnie was ready and dusted with sauce he put everything on a tray and retreated to his bedroom.

Once he had successfully climbed the three flights of stairs without spilling a drop of tea he placed the tray onto the bed and knelt down beside his record collection. He had one record in mind. Loz searched through his collection until he found what he was looking for; *'Taste of Pink'*. It was the only Prisoners album that he owned. Loz eagerly removed the vinyl from its sleeve and placed it onto the record deck. A few crackles later the aggressive mod garage sounds from The Prisoners plugged every gap in the bedroom. Loz surrendered himself to the frenzy of excitement that *'Better in Black'* whisked up. He took a bit of his cheese sarnie and washed it down with a gulp of sweet tea. His thoughts turned to The Prisoners gig that he would actually be going to.

The Prisoners were a band that lived only a few miles away in the nearby City of Rochester. Loz had tried several times to go and watch the band but for one reason or another each opportunity had fallen through. He felt optimistic about the forthcoming gig. He told himself that Den would not let him down. He twisted the volume knob up on the record player, shut his eyes and absorbed the music. Loz stayed in this position whilst the tracks *'Taste of Pink'* and *'Maybe I was wrong'* played.

As the fourth song on the album begun he jumped to his feet and stripped off to his Y fronts. Loz already knew what he was going to wear to the gig. He had been planning the outfit in his mind for days. Loz had even had a few nights where he had woken up full of anxiety as to what he should or should not wear. He already had the items piled up outside the wardrobe. He dived into his White jeans and pushed his feet into a pair of black suede Chelsea boots. Next he unfolded his favourite shirt which was a green and white Paisley pattern number and put it on. There was something about doing the buttons up on a cool shirt that always thrilled him. Loz then positioned himself in front of the mirror and combed his hair ensuring the parting on the left was immaculate. Then after a splash of aftershave and grabbing his blue denim jacket he turned off the record player and left the bedroom.

Loz swaggered to the Howard Wardell feeling the B's and E's. The streets were quiet and as he approached the youth club he heard Den's Vespa Sprint ticking over idly. Den noticed Loz strolling towards him and stuck his thumb up. Loz reciprocated by doing the same.

'Nice Chelsea boots,' Said Den which boosted Loz's confidence.

Den then handed Loz an open face crash helmet and nodded his chin towards the rear seat on his scooter. Loz put the helmet on as he straddled the scooter. The engine panels felt warm on his legs which he tried to protect from getting any oil of them. He then berated himself for choosing white jeans. Loz shuffled in the seat as Den revved the engine. Next Den released the bike stand and the scooter jerked forward. Loz nervously grabbed hold of Den's White Denim jacket. The first five minutes ride was the most frightening and then Loz calmed down and grew confident in Dens control of the Vespa.

Den yelled a few things from out of his full face crash helmet but Loz didn't understand. They rode up a steep hill where the scooter struggled and then rode pass Peneden Heath. A few groups of youths kicked footballs around and a few people supped beers in the garden of the Bull pub on the heath. It was a sunny pleasant evening. Loz felt cool sitting on the back of the scooter of one of the towns most respected Mods. He hoped to pass a few people that would recognise him. They rode pass a woodland area and down a steep hill. Den opened up the throttle and the scooter buzzed into life. Loz clutched Dens coat a bit tighter.

At the bottom of the hill Den pulled the scooter into a car park opposite a restaurant. The car park was half full of restaurant customers and the other half had approximately twenty Lambretta's and Vespa's. Many of the scooters carried passengers so Loz calculated that the number of Mods must be near thirty five. Den steered his Sprint in amongst the bikes and halted next to a purple 1961 Lambretta Ll series two and a rusting white Lambretta Jet. Charlie sat on the Jet and lifted the visor of his crash helmet.

'Good turnout ain't it?' observed Charlie, to which Den scanned the crowd and nodded.

'It's shaping up to be a good night. Has anyone checked to make sure The Prisoners are still playing tonight?' asked Den.

'Not that I know of but fuck it, it won't matter, we will still have a good time won't we?'

'Who's that on the Vespa?' enquired Den pointing his chin in the direction of a green and yellow Vespa.

'It's a friend of Micks. They rode over from Tonbridge. I don't know what the model is though.'

'It's a Vespa VBA,' Informed Den.

Both Charlie and Loz were impressed. Loz stepped off of the bike to stretch his legs. He removed his crash helmet and weaved in and around the scooters. He wanted to be seen. Loz received a few nods from some of the older Mods that were aware what happened regards the fight with the Skinheads. Loz felt more at ease in the older Mods company than he had ever done. Loz was still bathing in glory when he stumbled over and fell into a small frame Vespa. As he regained his balance he saw three mod girls glaring at him. They looked fabulous in their Alice bands and mini-skirts. Loz recognised them as being some of the girlfriends of some of the older Mods. Loz tried to compose himself and mumbled an apology. The girls continued to snarl at him. Just then Den called out to him and waved him to return. Loz felt relieved and scampered back to Den's scooter.

'I don't think anybody else is coming so shall we head off' said Charlie.

Den nodded, exchanged a few more words then revved the throttle a few more times. Within seconds the other scooterists realized that it was time to go and joined in with starting up and revving their engines. Loz jumped on the rear of Dens Vespa. The roar of the twenty scooters and smell of the two- stroke thrilled him. He felt a rush of excitement as he exited the car park knowing he was part of a convoy of scooters. Den and Charlie's scooter led the way. They raced down the road until the merged with the duel carriageway.

The convoy hogged the inside lane as they ascended the Bluebell Hill much to the annoyance of the other motorists. Most of the scooters managed the steep long hill with no difficulty but a few struggled and slowly got separated from the majority. Loz loved every second of the adventure. He had ridden on scooters before but never for such a long distance as he was now. Once the convoy triumphed over the hill they flew down the other side and exited the duel carriageway. They sped through narrow streets lined with narrow terrace houses. The smell of two stroke wafted through peoples open windows spoiling their pie and mash dinners.

For the last hundred yards Loz and Den rode at the front of the convoy. Loz felt brilliant as they arrived in style at the venue. The venue for the gig was a hotel. In front of the hotel entrance was a massive car park. The car park was packed full with scooters. Loz marvelled at the sight. It reminded him of the gathering of Mods down the arches in *'Quadrophenia'*. A few Mods huddled around their scooters chatting but it was evident that most had already gone inside of the venue.

Once inside the car park the convoy dispersed to find parking spaces. Den rode to the far end of the car park followed by Charlie and three other scooters. They parked up, stretched their arms and legs and headed for the hotel entrance. As Loz walked in Dens shadow it suddenly occurred to him that he may be too young to be allowed entry. This will be embarrassing he thought to himself and imagined the humiliation he would feel as the Mod girls sung the Madness song *'Embarrassment'* at him. Den seemed to pick up on Loz's anxiety but assured him that he would have no trouble getting in. Loz believed him.

Den led the way through the entrance and paid his admission of two pounds. Loz copied him ensuring that he avoided eye contact with the old woman collecting the entrance money. Den appeared to know many people and it took a few minutes just to move along a few metres. Just before the main doors Den stopped to greet a tall man and a shorter stockier man. They all seemed very pleased to see each other. 'This is Tim' introduced Den pointing to the taller man 'and this is Tiny' pointing to the other man. The two acknowledged Loz politely then continued to chat with Den. A few more seconds passed before they were joined by a girl with long blonde hair. She had pretty blue eyes and a pretty face and wore a yellow mini-skirt with suede knee length boots. Tim introduced the girls the name, but Loz didn't catch what it was because at that very moment the door swung open and the blast of music stamped out Tim's words. The girl pushed Loz who in turn pushed Den through the main doors.

Some nineteen sixties American garage music was playing. Loz scanned the room. It was packed full of Paisley and Polka dot shirt wearing boys and girls. Den headed for the bar and the girl followed pulling Loz by the sleeve of his denim jacket. They reached the crowded bar and Den yelled out what drinks did they want. The girl yelled back Snake bite and Loz nodded in agreement. Loz presumed he was one of the youngest in the room. It made him feel proud. The girl asked him how he knew Den and then she fired a volley of questions at him about Den. Loz twigged where her interest lay and did his best to answer her questions.

Den handed them their drinks and they moved away from the bar in search of a space to stand. The Dee jay played a few tunes that Loz recognised and to demonstrate that he knew the songs he jerked his back up and down to the songs. Den and the girl flirted with each other. Then the moment arrived. There was an eruption of pushing and shoving as the crowd realized that The Prisoners were walking onto the stage. Several boys whistled and cheered. A few girls squealed with delight.

Allan the bands bassist yelled something into the microphone to which the crowd applauded vigorously. Someone near the front called out to Allan but he responded with a dour expression. Loz got swept up by a group of Mods barging their way into the densest area of the crowd. He managed to squeeze through a few people until he found a spot that seemed less hectic. The crowd were wild and hungry.

Loz fixed his attention on the band members. He was stunned by their appearance. They each wore *Star Trek* uniforms. Graham the lead singer and guitarist and Allan wore red uniforms whilst Johnny the drummer and James the organ player wore blue. They each wore black trousers and black Chelsea boots. Loz had never witnessed anything like it. He thought they looked fantastic.

Graham strummed the first chord of *'Better in Black'* and the crowd went wild. The rest of the band joined in with the harsh attacking guitar sound and the song exploded in to life. Many members of the audience joined in with the singing and Loz joined in with them. The audience swayed from side to side. Loz tried to look over heads searching for Den but he couldn't see him. The punchy first song ended and the crowd roared in appreciation. Graham screamed something into the microphone but Loz didn't catch what he said. They then launched into their first instrumental track of the gig. Loz soaked up every second. He still couldn't believe that he was actually watching The Prisoners live.

Loz was still trying to convince himself that he was not dreaming when the band announced they were going to play their single *'Hurricane'*. The audience screamed loud as Graham's energetic stage presence dominated the stage. He looked volatile and unpredictable. Loz thought he had the look and presence of an angry young man. The singer treated the audience to his stage act which involved some posturing with his guitar and he that teased and intimated the onlookers. The crowd loved it. At one point Graham starred directly into Loz's eyes. He had a vivid intensity about him that Loz had only ever observed in Paul Weller.

The Prisoners continued to charge through their set at a high octane pace. They poured their unique garage mod rock onto their frenzied flock. The band played several songs that Loz didn't recognise but one in particular left a special impression on him. After the gig Loz discovered the title of the song was *'Love changes'*.

The audience had appeared to of doubled by the time the band performed their last song. The band dripped sweat over the crowd and their instruments. Allan continued to exchange words with the audience and Graham took large gulps from his pint glass. The last song ended abruptly and the band exited the stage. The audience cried out for more and Loz joined in with them. Like the others around him he was enjoying himself too much and was not ready for it to end. The crowd stood firm and continued to shout 'More, more, and more'. Then they erupted again as they saw Graham lead the band back onto the stage.

The Prisoners unleashed a further two raw and energetic songs onto the crowd to satisfy their hunger and they chewed up every last crumb until the band waved their goodbyes and slipped off back stage. The audience relaxed and gradually began to disperse. Loz wandered around until he caught sight of Den who had already seen him. Den waved him over and asked him what he thought.

'I'm speechless. That is the best thing I've ever seen,' said Loz.

Den grinned with the comment 'Yeah brilliant aint they. Well you can go back and tell your mates that you have The Prisoners now can't you'.

Loz couldn't wait. A few of the Mods that had been in the convoy with Den and Loz gathered around them. Den was too engrossed in the girl whom he had spent the entire gig chatting with to notice. Then Loz felt a sweaty body standing next to him. He turned around and saw Allan the Prisoners bassist standing beside him. Loz felt his mouth drop; his night was getting better and better. Allan offered a small smile, then tapped the girl Den was talking to on the arm. The girl turned around and smiled.

'Den, Loz, this is my brother Allan' she said.

Den shook Allan's hand and Loz followed. He did not care that Allan's hand was covered in sweat. Den informed Allan that he thought the gig was brilliant. He also told the bassist that it was the twelfth time that he had seen the band. Allan appeared impressed and thanked Den for his support. Allan then turned to Loz and asked him what he thought of the gig. Loz couldn't believe it. It was so unexpected he didn't have time to think and blurted out much to his embarrassment 'I love The Prisoners'. Allan simply smiled then continued to chat with his sister and Den.

WHEN YOU'RE YOUNG

Loz spent the next few days coming down from The Prisoners impressive performance. On leaving the gig he had snatched up flyers that advertised the bands future gigs. Most were in London but Loz knew he just had to see the band again, and soon.

The most energy that Loz had exerted since The Prisoners gig was a few hand jobs and few games of football at different locations. When Loz was younger he used to play most of his football on Peneden Heath but as he got older and mixed with new friendship groups at school, mainly the Mod's he gravitated to another place known as 'The Hut'.

The weather was still promising a long hot summer for Loz and his friends and so far he was enjoying every second of it. Loz was sitting at the kitchen table munching on a piece of toast dripping with butter. He was keenly scrutinising the pages of the newspaper that his dad had left lying around from the previous day. Loz was enjoying his leisurely morning and enjoying the peace and quiet in the household. He was dusting some crumbs off of his tee shirt when his mum entered the kitchen clutching a plastic bag which she placed gently beside the fridge.

'You okay Loz?' she enquired.

Loz nodded and bit off more toast.

'Guess who I saw in town,' she started, it annoyed Loz when people said that. Loz liked playing football, pool, the family's secret game called Black Magic which they only played at Christmas to tease his sister's new boyfriends, and Chess even but not Guess Who.

'I've no idea.'

'Maggie Potts. Do you remember her son? You went to St Paul's together. Well, she told me that Mathew has been sent to prison. Mind you she didn't tell me why, but she did say that they haven't spoken for a few years.'

Loz' mum continued to natter on but Loz drifted off into his own memories of Mathew. Loz never called him Mathew. He was known as Pottsy. The only recollection Loz had of Pottsy went back to when they were about six years old. Loz recalled arriving at school only to discover Pottsy being bathed by the head mistress. The headmistress had a metal tub half full of water and Pottsy was being scrubbed in it by her. The thing that Loz recalled however was that the metal bath was in the corridor of the school so everyone that passed witnessed Pottsy's humiliation. Loz had remembered feeling sorry for Pottsy back then. Pottsy had a reputation for being a smelly boy. He came from a poor deprived family nearby and was evidently neglected along with the several other siblings that he had.

Loz still had the image of Pottsy in his head when his mum asked him another question.

'Do you want to finish this up? I need to clear some space in the fridge.'

She then held out the last slice of the flying saucer cake. Loz accepted and dived into it. His mum finished filling the fridge with food and grabbed a basket full of clothes that were ready for ironing and took them upstairs. Loz licked the last bits of cream from his lips and returned to reading the newspaper.

An article on the momentum of the miner's strikes up North grabbed his attention. The images of down trodden, pissed off miners being addressed by an angry looking Arthur Scargill generated some interest in him. The article below showed a photograph of the 'Iron Lady' in all her glory and expensive tweed suit. Loz read the article desperately trying to empathise with the miners. However the more he tried the more he found that he couldn't relate to their issues. Loz didn't know any miners. He had never met any miners. Loz had never even seen a mine. He wished the miners luck with their protests and took another sip of his tea feeling grateful that he lived down South.

Loz nonchalantly continued to flick through the pages until he came across a photograph of Neil Kinnock. It was not the picture of Kinnock that caught his attention but the photograph of his son and paragraph that revealed that Kinnocks son was an active participant in the football casual movement. Loz perked up. Loz eagerly read the article which appeared to be having a dig at Kinnock for allowing his son to spend so much 'Labour' money on expensive items of clothing. Loz was not especially interested by the argument. Instead he was captivated by the photograph of Kinnocks son clad from head to toe in his finest designer sportswear.

Loz thought the young man looked the 'dog's bollocks' in his V-neck sweater with a Golden Eagle badge on the breast, a pair of trousers with slits in the them that hung over a pair of clean White trainers. The picture of Kinnocks son reminded Loz of the mannequin in 'Hucks'. The article informed that Kinnocks son had been spotted hauling carrier bags out of a shop called 'Simons' in Shepherds Bush. The article continued saying that 'Simons' was the mecca for all aspiring casuals. The shop appeared to be the epicentre of all things casual. It was the place to go and see and be seen.

Loz read the article a second time and scrutinised every detail of the clothing that Kinnocks son wore. Once satisfied that he had memorised everything he grabbed the list of chores that his mum had bestowed onto him. Chore one read cut the grass, chore two was hoover the living room and bathroom and the final chore was scribbled in bold capital letters, FIND A JOB. Loz chuckled and screwed up the list. He knew that at least two of the chores were impossible.

An hour later Loz was washing the grass stains off his hands and splashing some of his dad's aftershave over himself. Loz left the house dressed in his army combats, polo shirt and Deck shoes. The distance to the hut was considerably further than that of the heath but he had arranged to see friends there. Loz decided to take the shortcut via the army barracks. He left the house and took the street where Bowie had allegedly lived for a while.

A few yards in front of him a man and woman walked out of their front door. Loz recognised the young woman as Julie, Loz vaguely knew her older brother. The man with her was one of the local soul boys. He was a typical soulie dressed in tea bag tee shirt, pegged trousers and jelly shoes. The couple argued with each other as they walked towards the males Capri. Loz didn't pay much attention until he heard the slapping sound of the man's hand as it struck Julie around the face. Loz was shocked and slowed his pace. Julie fell silent and obedient and got quietly into the Capri. As Loz passed the car the driver shot Loz a menacing stare. It chilled Loz to the bone as he hurried down the street a host of emotions seethed through his blood stream. It was the first time he had witnessed a man hit a woman. Loz felt sorry for Julie and disgusted with the man.

Loz continued to walk down the street towards a shortcut that he often used that took him through the local army barracks. The image of the man hitting Julie replayed in his mind making his blood boil. He had been in such a good mood and it was at risk of being shattered. To counteract this Loz reminded himself of the first time he attempted to be fashionable. It had been just after he had seen the film *'Grease'*. Loz had asked his mum to get him a plain white tee shirt and a comb. For weeks he pretended to be John Travolta wearing his white tee shirt and jeans which he slipped the comb into the rear pocket. The memory and innocence of it cheered him up.

Loz turned right at the bottom of the street and continued to climb up the slope towards the barracks. He pictured himself many years earlier making the same walk. Only this time he and his friends were collecting the wood spikes from fireworks. Every year on the morning after fireworks night Loz and his friends would search the streets gathering up the wood spikes. It was their competition to see who found the most.

On the left was the Iron gates of the Primary school Loz had attended after St Paul's. The school was a collection of single storey low rise brick buildings. The caretaker lived with his family in a cottage near the entrance. Loz never knew his name even though he must have passed him a thousand times either around the corridors of the school, the playground or whilst he pottered around in his beautiful flowery garden.

Loz paused for a moment to peer through the unattended gate. His eyes followed the path that led to the entrance way and he wondered how many times in the four or five years that he attended the school that he must of walked down that path. Not on Mondays though he chuckled to himself as a memory gate crashed his thoughts. There had been a time where Loz had fabricated illnesses. However, after the third dose Loz's mum 'twigged' that something was wrong and it was nothing to do with being ill. She enquired what the real problem was and Loz admitted that the reason he did not want to go to school on Mondays was because the teacher had introduced Maths tests. Loz hated Maths. He was no good at it and it worried him so much that he fabricated the illnesses in an attempt to avoid the maths tests. Loz's mum spoke to the teachers and the following Monday he went to school and 'got on' with it. Loz tutted reminding himself that he was still rubbish when it came to anything mathematical.

Loz walked closer to the school gates and stuck his nose through the gaps in the railings and wrapped his fingers around them. A few moments and faces from his time during the school flashed through his mind. He remembered that it was in the school that he was introduced to his first girlfriend. Claire her name was. She tiny, pretty thing with long blonde hair and blue eyes. Loz could not actually remember asking her out, but recalled that they were just kind of thrown together. His first girlfriend lasted two weeks.

Loz pictured moments of running around the playground and playing marbles on the drain grids in the playground. There were only three grids in the playground so the chances of getting a game were always a challenge. He then reminded himself that it was in the playground that he found himself on the end of his first head butt. Loz could not recall why he had been assaulted by the head butter but he did recall that it had hurt and had brought a tear to his eye that he attempted to disguise.

Loz then strained to catch a glimpse of the large playing field that lay behind the school. He had very fond memories of playing in the school field during the seemingly endless sunny days. He especially enjoyed playing amongst the redundant air raid shelters that remained in the playing field and on other areas of the school premises. To his knowledge they had been used in the last war to protect the school children and anyone else that could reach them in time. The air raid shelters were cold and damp inside and during his school years had only served as storage space for old school chairs and tables.

But Loz's most favourite memory of the school playing field related to the time that he started up an exclusive gang called 'The Cossacks'. Because Loz had started the gang up he had naturally been declared the leader too. Loz loved the title and responsibility of being the leader and took his role as serious as any nine year boy could. One of his first tasks was to write a chant that could be sung by the other members. The song had a simple tune that could be easily remembered by the less bright members and the words were even simpler 'We are the Cossacks, we are the Cossacks'. This would be chanted repeatedly until the gang ran out of energy or simply got bored.

Loz the leaders other responsibility was deciding who was allowed to join The Cossacks exclusive gang. Again this was a simple process. No girls. Loz had no reasoning behind the decision but it was agreed and he remembered that the girls even went off to start their own exclusive gang. This led to the two gangs declaring war upon each other so Loz decided he needed to provide his troops with weapons.

Loz ran home after school and into the 'Home Brew' shop two doors down from his home. Loz had an idea. The shop sold see through plastic tubes that were used in the wine making process. The woman in the shop tried to explain to Loz what the plastic tubes were for. Something to do with sucking the wine out or letting air into the glass containers, Loz recalled but he never really understand their real use. Loz left the shop a metre of tube and went home.

Once home he found a sharp knife and cut sections of the tube into six inch lengths. He took the tubes to school the following morning and distributed them amongst his loyal troops. The Cossacks looked at him confused. What could they possibly do with six inch plastic tubes? Loz led them to the playing field and told them to gather around round him. After a couple of chants of 'We are the Cossacks, we are the Cossacks' Loz picked up a flea dart from amongst the grassy field. He split the dart in two and popped one into the plastic tube. He then blew one end of the tube and the dart flew out and stuck to the hair of another passing by pupil. The Cossacks caught on and set about gathering ammunition. They stuffed their pockets with flea darts and once confident that they had enough for a war ran off to find the girl gang. Of course Loz led the charge and chanting. The memory bought back a warm feeling and Loz smiled inside. He released the bars of his former prison and walked on up the hill.

As Loz approached the entrance to the barracks he spotted the tall wooden post which had a green metal siren fastened to the top of it. The siren was a relic left over from the Second World War. However the locals suspected the siren remained to warn them of an atomic attack from the Russians. Loz had grown up accepting the possibility of it. Loz entered the narrow alley way and saw two soldiers guarding the entrance. They held rifles and wore their camouflage uniforms and helmets. The guards allowed Loz to pass without battering an eye lid. The soldiers were used to young people using the short cut through the barracks to either visit friends whose parents were squaddies or simply to get to the other side of town.

Loz casually strolled through the streets of the barracks passing several armoured vehicles, tanks and squaddies going about their business. Loz always found the barracks to be an interesting but eerie place. The barracks housed several thousand soldiers and their families in what appeared to be smallish terraced houses. Over the years Loz had befriended many kids who lived in the barracks. Some stayed for many years and some for only a few months. Loz was pleased that he didn't have to endure the life of a soldier's child. Their dads always seem to be tough, disciplined men, plus they moved around too much for Loz.

Loz skirted the Naafi which was the area where the soldiers ate and drank, he exited the main gates of the barracks, nodding to the armed guards as he did and found himself standing on the edge of an extremely busy main road.

After waiting patiently for a break in the flow of traffic Loz grabbed his opportunity and scampered across the road to the other side. He had the choice to go left or right to get to the hut. For no particular reason he chose left. Loz ambled through the

Nineteen Fifties council estate until he came upon a small car park. This led to a narrow gap in the hedges which in turn led to a wide grassy field. About a hundred yards on the far side of the field was the painted white wooden hut. The hut was the changing rooms for the home and away teams that used the football pitch on the field. The local footy team was 'The Colts'. Loz had played for 'The Colts' a couple of seasons previously and via them he had actually been invited to have trials with his own towns under Fifteen's football team. Loz had not been successful in the trials but was still able to brag about at least getting trials for years to come. 'The Colts' played in light blue and white stripy kit. Loz favoured the colours.

Loz headed directly for the hut passing under one of the set of goal posts. There were no net's, the nets were only attached on match days. As Loz walked under the square posts it occurred to him how much it would hurt the players to go smashing into them. He found it odd that he had never considered this before especially as his position had been the winger and so had spent many moments in the goal mouth.

There were a few young people congregated around the hut. A couple of them waved as Loz got nearer. Neil and his brother Paul were sitting on the lowest step of the hut setting fire to pieces of paper. Looking over their shoulders was a tiny framed Skinhead girl whose name was Tanya. Her feather cut hairstyle was in need of some tender loving care. Behind Tanya sat her closest friend Dani. Dani was a chubby black girl who dressed like she belonged in the two tone band The Bodysnatchers. Loz had a lot of time for Dani. She had been in and out of fostering since her early childhood. Loz never heard her talk about her blood parents. Loz admired the way she remained cheerful. Sitting on the step next to Dani was a boy the same age as Paul. His name was Daz.

Daz was sporting a scruffy pair of burgundy sta-prest, scuffed Loafers and a grubby tee shirt that had a photograph of The Chords on it. Daz was holding court by dangling one of his ferrets in front of the group.

Loz did what he could to avoid Daz. The two never really saw eye to eye on matters. Also, Loz didn't feel like he could trust him. Loz took the position to keep his distance as much as possible. Even more so when Daz brought out his ferrets to show off with. The arrival of Loz diverted some of the attention away from Daz and his pet. Loz noticed that this annoyed him so he hastily greeted everyone and turned his own attention to the ferret.

Daz resumed and built up the climax which included shoving the pet down his trousers and letting it run down the inside of his leg. Tanya cheered and the others fell about laughing. Then as the ferret reappeared Daz grabbed it by the scruff of its neck and pounced onto Neil. Neil in turn tried to escape the fate of having to deal with the ferret hooking its sharp teeth into his testicles. Again the group laughed and Tanya cheered. Neil resisted long enough for Daz to give up. Everything calmed down.

'Fancy a kick about?' asked Neil rolling the football along the ground towards Loz.

'Yeah, go on then' replied Loz and the two jogged over to the nearest set of goal post passing the ball back and forth as they did so. Tanya followed. She had a reputation as being a bit of a tom boy. A few minutes later Paul also joined in. Daz went home to feed the ferret. For the next hour the group of friends played headers and volleys together.

After an hour Loz decided he needed a rest and a drink. He told the others he was going to disappear for a while but might return later. Then he waved his goodbyes and walked away from the hut. It was only a five minute walk to his friend's council house. On his arrival he simply opened the front door and entered inside. The custom was to do this. Loz often wondered if the family who lived in the house ever locked the front door.

The room was its usual smelly and smokey self. The smoker was the father of Loz's friend Jim. Old Mac was an elderly Irish man that had come to live in England in the mid-Fifties. Mac was a short and wiry man and always wore a Trilby hat. Mac smoked like a trooper. It was a habit that his only son Jim was fast picking up on. Jim was also short with jet black hair. It was obvious he had Irish blood in him. Jim was bent over the pool table that took up most of the space in the room. Loz could barely make out the colour of the balls on the table through the thick smoke. Jim's opponent was a tall skinny boy who also lived on the estate. His name was Chaz. Chaz always seemed to wear a blue V-neck jumper, grey sta-prest trousers and Desert boots. They all greeted one another and Loz found a spot to stand in one of the corners of the room.

Every so often Mac would mumble something about his son's pool playing skills but he spoke in such a quiet but thick Irish accent that Loz never understood a word. Even though Loz had known Mac for a few years he reckoned he could probably count the amount of words he had understood Mac say on one hand.

Whilst the boys played pool and old Mac puffed away The Jam album 'Setting Sons' had been playing in the background. As the record played Loz recalled listening to the album whilst watching Jim and Chaz playing on the same pool table during the summer holidays the year before. After that particular holiday 'Setting Sons' became Loz's favourite Jam album.

Loz had fond memories of that misspent summer holiday. He had spent a great deal of it hanging out with Jim and Chaz. In between playing pool and sucking in Macs cigarette smoke 'Setting Sons' was played over and over again. Loz learnt virtually every lyric sung by Weller. The album had a great feel to Loz. It was rich and warm but retained its youthful aggressiveness. 'Thick as thieves' and 'Saturdays kids' had summed up Loz's life during that period. That summer holiday was also especially hot so between games of pool and The Jam the three friends would head off to cool down by the river and fish. Loz learnt to fish during those holidays but after that never held another fishing rod. In truth, he found the sport boring.

Loz stayed and watched Jim and Chaz play pool for half an hour before deciding he could inhale no more fag smoke. He said his goodbyes and left. Loz wandered back to the hut where the crowd of youth had swelled to around twenty. Daz had also returned. Only this time he had two ferrets with him. Loz had a brief chat with Dani and Tanya about leaving school for good. Daz was teasing some of the younger kids with the ferrets that looked like they wanted blood. Loz and Neil decided it was time to evacuate so quietly slid away from the ensuing chaos and headed off in the direction of town.

There were two routes available to town from the hut. One meant walking alongside the busy main road at the top of the estate and the other route was a narrow dusty path that ran beside the river. Loz and Neil decided there was no rush so they chose the river side route. Plus it was going to be quieter than the main road and this appealed to Loz. As they strolled along the path they conversed about the fight with the Skinheads down the Wander Inn. It was the first real opportunity they had had to discuss it.

'Do you think Webby and that lot know who we are yet?' asked Neil.

'Dunno Neil, it's hard to say.'

'It's only a matter of time though isn't it? I mean if they ask enough people they will find out our names and where we hang out.'

'If they are that bothered. You have to remember they are a lot older than us and have probably already forgotten us'. Loz tried to sound hopeful.

'Fuck off Loz. We humiliated them. They are not going to forget that a bunch of young Mods gave as good as they got. I don't care how many old boilers they have been banging since the ruck I still think they will want to bang the shit out of us.'

'Yeah, I know. Best we can do is keep our heads down, don't brag about it and keep our fingers crossed that it gets forgotten about in time.'

For a while they walked in silence. Loz liked that about Neil and his relationship. There was no urgency, no need to fill the silences with idle chatter. Loz listened to the birds singing. He liked the summery feel that birds created when they sung. A few narrow boats and other small craft passed them. The would be captains smoked their pipes and waved at them. The two boys ignored them. Neil asked Loz if he had watched the *Spitting Image* episode from the previous night. Loz said he hadn't and the conversation ended there. There was more silence before Neil asked Loz if he knew about the trip to London that the Howard Wardell was organising. Loz hadn't heard of it so Neil explained that the trip would include a visit to both Pettycoat Lane market and Carnaby Street. Neil informed Loz that if he wanted to go he had to phone Dave from the youth club and book his place. Loz said he would do it as soon as he got home.

The two walked on for another ten minutes until they walked under a large iron bridge. Only trains going to and from London used it. Beside the bridge was a metal staircase that they climbed up. From the staircase they walked through a long passage way. They needed to keep their wits about them because the passage way was a regular haunt for the Skinheads and Punks to glue sniff from. They reached the end of the passageway without spotting a single bone head or Mohican. They had to step over many white plastic bags though which the Punks and Skinheads had discarded after they had sniffed the glue out of them.

On exiting the passageway they entered a public gardens area. The area was well maintained. The epicentre of the gardens was an old Edwardian band stand. Loz had never seen it used by any musicians though. Only the children and occasional drunk made use of it. The band stand still looked ornate and impressive. The band stand reminded Loz of The Jam's *When you're young* video.

'Did I ever tell you?' begun Loz 'the story of the time my neighbour and me found a bunch of dirty mags down here?'

Neil shook his head.

'It was just there, in those bushes. We were gathering up conkers actually and strayed from the path to search behind the bushes. It was then that we found a collection of dirty mags. We looked through them both feeling a bit naughty and a bit embarrassed. I always remember that some of the pages had been ripped and some pictures had been torn out' explained Loz.

'What did you do with them? Did you keep them?' enquired Neil.

we did about them. May be we just left them there for the next dirty old man to have a five finger hand shuffle over.'

The two of them burst into laughter .They weaved between the well maintained flower beds and park benches until they stumbled over an enclosed area surrounded by flowery bushes. In the centre of the area was a square shape pond. On each side of the pond was a stone bench upon which some of the local tramps were lounging in the sunshine. Nobody seemed to know the tramps real names so everyone knew them by their nicknames. Loz and Neil recognised two of the tramps as being 'Pig Bin Billy' and the 'Mustard Man'.

Townsfolk believed that 'Pig Bin Billy' was the son of a wealthy businessman and would have been heir to a fortune. However, rumour had it that he had been estranged from his family since the late Sixties and had roamed the streets collecting his meals from bins around the town ever since. He was often seen leaning over bins and that's how he got the name. The 'Mustard Man' got his name because he always pushed a trolley with a bag that advertised an English Mustard on it. That bag seemed to last forever. The 'Mustard Man' was short and hobbled along. Unlike the other tramps he actually had a place to live. He lived in a street not far from Loz and most nights he could be heard screaming and yelling in the dark of night. Story had it that he had been a soldier in the last war and a bomb had exploded near to him. The experience left the young man in a state known as shell shocked. Forty years later the poor man still suffered the effects of it.

The tramps contributed to the fabric of the town. They were harmless and the townsfolk tolerated them. On the whole they kept themselves to themselves so nobody spared them a thought. There were half a dozen areas that the tramps frequented to stay out of sight. The pond area of the park gardens was one of them. Loz and Neil ambled up to the edge of the pond. The tramps didn't bat an eyelid and simply continued to ramble on to each other and sip from their bottles of cheap wine. Loz didn't notice Neil unzip his trousers, pull out his cock and start pissing in the pond. Suddenly the tramps erupted into a frenzy of abuse. They staggered to their feet and swayed from side to side. Neil hurried his piss and Loz took a few steps back. Neil spilt piss onto his hands and legs as he darted away from the angry tramps. As the two boys backed off they could hear one of the tramps yelling 'Oi, how would you like it if I came and took a piss in your front room.'

Loz and Neil ran off to a safe distance laughing. They knew full well the tramps had a point though after all that pond area probably did seem like their front room. They found a spot under a massive old English Oak tree and ogled at the girls passing by before they fell asleep in the shade.

ANGELS AND DIRTY FACES

'Err, for fucks sake!' cried Loz looking at the glowing red numbers on the digital clock. It was twelve thirty and he had been fast asleep in bed since ten o clock. Loz pulled the sheet covers up over his head and hissed more curses at his next door neighbour. Micky was the older brother of Pete. He also had his bedroom built into the converted attic area. This meant that Micky's room was exactly next to Loz's. Only a couple of bricks separated them. Micky had a habit of returning home from the pub and in his inconsiderate drunken state play records inappropriately loud. Loz had needed to put up with it since nineteen seventy seven. The only respite Loz had was after Micky fell out with his mum, Pauline, and moved to a friend's house for a few weeks. Sadly for Loz this didn't happen enough.

Micky had recently spit up from his long term girlfriend of nine months and had been out getting drunk every other night. On this occasion Micky returned home from the pub with his old school mate Andy. Loz could hear they were in high spirits and spat more curses at them knowing it was going to be a long night. After a few minutes of loud talking and giggling they cranked up the music. The Sex Pistols shook the bedroom walls. Loz had grown to like the Sex Pistols after having spent many days and nights listening to Micky play songs by the band. Micky and Andy had been original punks, and whilst Micky retained his scruffy punkish look Andy had moved on to a more Gothic appearance.

Loz wrapped his pillow around his head as the Sex Pistols moved aside allowing several songs from The Clash and then The Buzzcocks to assault the midnight hour. Laughter and giggles continued and then Loz realized that there was also a girl with them. Loz strained his ears trying to work out if she was alone or with a friend. Her giggles got louder as Andy took over the record player, 'bollocks' sighed Loz as Soft Cells version of the brilliant Northern Soul classic 'Tainted Love' begun. Then when it had finished it was played again, and then again and then again countless times.

Loz had eventually drifted back off to sleep because the next time he awoke the red glowing numbers on the clock said eight twenty. Despite having a shit night's sleep Loz felt energised. He stood on his bed and opened the blind on the sky light window and pushed the window open a few inches. The cool breeze felt good as it gushed into the bed room. Loz took a few deep breaths of the fresh air then fell back onto his bed. The fresh air excited him. In his mind he tried to picture the girls from Wham and Bananarama but he found it hard to settle on which one he fantasised over the most. The blonde girl won. The image of the blonde girl dissolved and faded and he got out of bed a happier young man and ready to take the day on.

There was nothing in particular that Loz needed to do. There was nowhere he especially needed to be so he took each moment as it presented itself. At around noon he wandered down the hut but there was nobody there. He considered dropping by Jim's house for a game of pool and fill his lungs with smoke but at the last moment he changed his mind and went to see if Robert was in. Robert opened the door wearing only a soaking wet pair of jeans.

'What the fuck are you doing?' asked Loz.

'I'm trying to shrink my new jeans so that they fit me perfectly.'

Loz laughed then stepped inside. He followed Robert and his dripping jeans to the front room.

'Ah, that's where you got the idea,' said Loz noticing the television screen had the frozen image of Jimmy in 'Quadrophenia' drumming along to 'My Generation' and wearing his wet jeans.

'Are you staying for a bit? Coz if you are I'll rewind the video and you can watch it with me whilst my jeans dry.'

Loz shrugged his shoulders and accepted the offer. He plonked down on the arm chair whilst Robert sat on a towel on the floor. Loz had been too young to see 'Quadrophenia' at the cinema but he had watched it many times on video. He loved the film with its characters, clothes and music. It was his favourite film, plus he would give anything to be in Jimmy's shoes up the alley in Brighton. Watching the film also killed a couple of hours.

At three o clock Loz left Roberts and popped down to see his Nan where he drank tea and swallowed crumpets. He passed his Uncle Ron on the way out and returned home for his tea. Loz found his sister watching Abba perform 'Dancing Queen' on the television. Loz always associated the song with his sister. When they very young he once found her prancing around the living room to the song. The image of his sister dancing cemented itself in his mind and whenever he heard the song he thought of her.

'Is dad home?' enquired Loz.

'No, he got some extra over time so won't be back until eight. Why?' she asked suspiciously.

'I was going to ask him to lend me a couple of quid coz I'm skint. Any chance....'

Loz's sister interrupted him with a sharp 'No.'

'Where's mum and tubby then?'

'Mum's taken him to the pictures. They should be home soon. You might as well sort your own tea out though.' She shot him a stern look.

Loz had half an hour to spare so he quickly made himself some cheese on toast which he smothered in sauce before having a shower and splashing aftershave over his chin. He dressed himself in his beloved cycling shirt, white Jean's and black Jam cycling shoes. He then headed for Isabel's house.

Isabel opened the door looking stunning in a yellow shift dress and white dolly shoes. She wore an Alice band in her hair. Isabel invited Loz inside. Isabel's house was decorated like it was frozen in the nineteen sixties. The walls were painted a mixture of yellow's, oranges and green's and all the furniture was from the sixties. Loz liked the retro feel of her house. There was no mod con's in it. It had something simple about it that Loz admired.

Loz sat in one of the chairs beside the glass dining room table. Isabel knelt on the floor and turned on her Dansette record player. She picked out The Jam album *'All mod con's'* and placed it carefully on the deck. The first song began.

'Good choice,' commented Loz.

'Yep, I've been playing this album loads recently.'

'So what have you been up to this week?' Loz asked.

'Not much really but I did have a letter arrive yesterday about that job interview I went to a couple of weeks ago.'

'Oh yeah, and?'

'They have offered me the job.' Isabel sounded pleased.

'Brilliant. Just remind me what job it was again.'

'The one down the newsagent's in the Stoneborough centre, remember,' She tutted.

Loz said he was pleased for her and they continued to chat about the job, her wages, and the perks. They were still discussing this when *'English Rose'* began. They both remained quiet whilst the song played. Loz observed Isabel throughout the song. She looked pretty in her yellow dress. Loz thought it complimented her dark hair and complexion. Her rosy cheeks stood out.

'So, what about you? What you been up to?' she asked once *'English Rose'* faded.

Loz rambled on for ten minutes about how wonderful The Prisoners gig had been. He told her about the ride over to the gig on the back of Dens Vespa and how much he had enjoyed that. Loz also made Isabel laugh when he recounted the story of the tramps down the gardens. Loz was still sharing his experiences when they left the house so they could go and meet some other friends.

They walked down the road towards the Howard Wardell but just before it they climbed over a wall and fell into a small children's play area. Robert and Neil were already waiting. They were sitting on the swings idly dangling their legs. They exchanged greetings before setting off in the direction of the Friday night Trinity Church disco.

'Is Theresa coming tonight' asked Robert looking at Loz.

Loz shrugged his shoulders and answered 'I dunno.'

'If she does are you going to get off with her again?'

Isabel, Neil and Robert all stared at Loz waiting for his response. Loz grinned and said that he may do.

'She really fancies you.' Isabel said 'Why don't you ask her out properly?'

Loz felt uncomfortable discussing the matter of Theresa so openly. He tried to disguise it and said 'I may do, I may not. There's plenty more fish in the sea'.

Isabel shook her head but Neil and Robert giggled. Within ten minutes they had reached the ground of the Trinity church. The actual church itself was old and austere looking. It had a high steeple. The church had been abandoned for several years. Loz never remembered it actually being used a place of worship in his lifetime. The graveyard was neglected as was the church. Loz's group weaved their through the moss covered, crumbling head stones and joined a larger group of youths standing near the main entrance of the church.

The collection of young people displayed a host of styles of fashions. The flight jackets, parkas and Harrington's mixed with Ra Ra skirts and *'Frankie Says'* baggy tee shirts. There were French line haircuts, feather cut's, skinheads and bleached hair. There were Jam shoes, Jelly shoes and high heeled stilettos.

Loz's group dispersed and mingled with other friends. Loz was joined by two friends he knew from school Carl and Nigel. They chatted for a while before Nigel produced a handful of tiny Blue and Green pills.

'What are they?' said Loz staring at the pills.

'Blues and Greens like the Mods use to take in the sixties,' informed Carl.

'Here have a couple?' offered Nigel.

'No you're alright' said Loz backing away. He had never seen a drug in his life and had no intention of accepting the pills. Carl and Nigel appeared put out and walked away. Loz found Isabel and told her about what he had been offered. Isabel assured him that he had done the right thing. They then made their way to the entrance where they paid their admission fee of fifty pence and they entered the enormous belly of the derelict church.

To their right was a high wooden stage where the Dee jay and his record player were positioned. The church still had its magnificent wooden parquet flooring. It was perfect to dance on. There was the high roof area that looked in desperate need of repair and the whole area was dark and gloomy. Only a few disco lights dispersed the moodiness of the old church.

As Loz and Isabel skirted the dance floor UB40's reggae classic *'Tyler'* was thumping out of the speakers. It was the twelve inch version that Loz loved and owned. The 'tribes' were already gathering in their adopted areas of the venue. The Mods gathered in one corner, the New Romantics in another, then the Bread heads had their area and next to them the Gothics and then Psychobilly's. No tribe strayed into one of the others tribe's portion of the disco. Each tribe took their turn on the dance floor as the Dee jay played a few tunes that fitted their genre. The disco was a shared experience in this manner and all obeyed the rules.

Loz led the way avoiding the other tribes as best he could until they joined their friends in the Mods corner. Tina and Dani were snogging the faces off of a couple of the older Mods. Neil and Paul were arguing over something like brothers like to argue. Loz scanned the room. He was impressed by the attendance. He also spotted a few characters that had fearful reputations. He sensed there may be some trouble brewing.

Over the next hour the Dee jay provided an eclectic mixture of songs that included *'Spellbound'* by Siouxsie and the Banshees, *'Ghost'* Japan, *'Sixty eight guns'* by the Alarm, *'Geno'* Dexys Midnight Runners, *'Girls just wanna have fun'* Cyndi Lauper, *'I feel for you'* Chaka Khan and *'Fields of Fire'* from Big Country. To keep Loz and his tribe happy the Dee jay spun *'Footsee'* by Wigan's chosen few, *'Tainted Love'* Gloria Jones, *'There's a ghost in my house'* by R. Dean Taylor, *'Solid bond in your heart'* The Style council and *'Green Onions'* from Booker T and the MG's.

When *'Green Onions'* was replaced by The Cramps the Psychobilly's rushed to the dance floor knocking a few Mods out of the way at the same time. They pushed and pulled one another whilst trying to avoid messing up their flat tops. Loz thought the sight of them was comical. The Dee jay only played a couple of songs by The Stray Cats before swapping to something that appealed to the New Romantics. Loz watched the Psychobilly's march off into their dark corner and be replaced by a group of girls who threw their hand bags onto the floor and danced around them in a circle.

Theresa was one of these girls. Loz's eyes followed her every move as she swayed her arse from side to side. She looked beautiful. She made for nice eye candy too and it sweetened his desire for another round with her. Loz's gaze was fixed on her when she suddenly turned and glanced at him. Loz quickly looked away. He sense that she was trying to catch his eye but he refused to look back at her. He didn't know why he was playing hard to get. Loz told himself he was being foolish. He knew he liked her. He also told himself that if he played his cards right he could get his cock sucked again. Loz shot Theresa a brief smile then faded in to the darkness of the Mod's corner where he found a seat and slumped down.

Loz looked around the room at all the kids having fun. He had known most of them for a long time. Apart from the occasional scuffle, everybody tolerated everyone else. His gaze fell onto his Mod friends surrounding him.

He felt proud of them and proud that he had chosen the Moddy route.

Being a Mod for Loz had begun when he was eleven years old. He had been dragged to the local Civil Service club that was the home and retreat to many Postmen, Prison Officers and their families. It was a place where the adults supped their subsidised beers, played Pool, Darts or Dominoes and the children blew bubbles into their pop and chomped bags of Skips. The entertainment included regular disco's, comedians and the annual children's christmas party with fairy cakes, balloons, clowns and some poor kid being sick in the corner.

But, it was on one particular disco night that Loz's attention was drawn towards a certain young male. The young man in question wore a crisp white button down shirt with a narrow black tie. He also wore a red V-neck jumper, dark blue jeans and beige desert boots. Loz had been impressed by the boy's appearance and the way he danced to 'Geno' and spent the night watching him. Following this Loz did some research and discovered that the look was that associated with something called Mod.

Loz did not understand the mystery behind his attraction to the look. On the surface it looked cool, sharp, smart. Only later did he discover that the look reflected the music that the 1960's Mod's liked. That was a whole new world that awaited Loz's discovery.

Loz asked his mum questions and she told him what she knew and remembered about the Mods in her own teens in the Sixties. She also showed Loz some old photographs of herself as a teenager with strange dyed hair, cool looking outfits and sitting on boyfriends Vespa's. Loz was amazed and impressed that his mum had actually been fashionable. He knew she took pride in her appearance and she kept up to date with the classic look of the times but he had not considered her to be hip in the Sixties.

Loz begged, borrowed and stole enough money so that by the time he returned to the next Civil Service disco he was clad in the same clothes as the young male he had seen the time before. Fortunately that particular boy was not at the disco so Loz could strut around like a peacock feeling like he stood out. He felt he had merged with fashion.

'Come on' said one of the older Mod's brushing past Loz and heading for the dance floor. A Northern Soul classic 'Right track' by Billy Butler had started and demanded that they dance. Loz complied and followed his tribe into war on the dancefloor. Loz joined in with the twenty or so dancers who remained twisting and turning to the music for a further four songs. As soon as 'London calling' started the Mod's exited the dance floor and three Punks fell into the spaces left. They looked like they had been sniffing glue. The Punks committed themselves to the next two songs 'God save the queen' and 'The kids are united'. Loz and his friends watched on whilst laughing at the Punk's performance.

Loz returned to the same seat he had been sat on before he had danced. He looked up to see that Theresa and some of her friends had merged with the Mod group. Theresa was chatting with Isabel. The two girls laughed, smiled and giggled. Occasionally Theresa glanced at him. Loz wondered if the girls were discussing him. He trusted that Isabel would be saying nice things about him. Loz tried to remain aloof though.

Loz looked over the girl's shoulders to get a better view of a lonely figure dancing on the far side of the dance floor. The song playing Loz recognised as 'Rockit' by Herbie Hancock. The song had been getting lots of radio air play recently. The lone figure of a young boy jerked his body to the drum beats. The boy danced in a manner that Loz had never witnessed before, it was robot like and mechanical. Loz was not sure what to make of it.

Loz strained to see what the boy was wearing. He was dressed different to mostly everyone else in burgundy jumbo cords, blue boots and a black tracksuit top with a letter 'T' in a circle over the breast area. He was a tallish, thick set boy and he had his dark hair styled in a wedge with a long fringe.

Loz recognised the boy as being from his old school. The boy had only attended a few months having only relocated to Kent from Bradford in Yorkshire. Loz had passed him in the school corridors a few times without exchanging a word. Loz did remember that the boy had been involved in a fight during his first week at the school. It was the norm. A new boy was someone for the hardest boys in the school to lay their claim to. That particular fight had been arranged to take place on the friday afternoon straight after school on the top field where the sponsored walk took place. The new boy and one of the schools tough nuts called Pete fought it out for five minutes before the fight was declared a draw. The new boy had stood his ground, given a good account of himself and after that had been accepted.

Loz was curious to find out more about the clothes the boy was wearing and why was he dancing like a spastic on acid. The boy was only given one song to dance to as the Dee jay removed 'Rockit' and played *Mirror in the bathroom* by The Beat instead. Loz ambled over to the other side of the dance floor and introduced himself to the boy with an 'Alright, I've seen you around school.'

The boy looked Loz up and down suspiciously before replying in a thick, broad Yorkshire accent 'Alright, yeah I recognise you too.'

'What's your name?' asked Loz.

'Gary. What's your name?'

'Loz. What was that dancing all about then?'

'It's called body popping. It goes with the music, you know Hip Hop.' Gary informed.

Loz looked extremely bemused then Gary continued 'Have you seen the film *Breakdance*? It's the music in the film. It's the new thing coming in. Keep your eye out for the Breakdancing, Hip Hop and Body popping.'

'It might be big up North, but it's not catching on down South.' returned Loz.

'It will. It's going to be massive Loz.' He sounded convincing.

Loz stood talking with Gary when they were joined by another boy who also had a long fringe wedge, only it was a spectacular Blonde. This boy was skinny and had a large nose and chisel shape chin. He wore faded jeans with white trainers and a yellow tee shirt with a blue crocodile badge on the breast. The boy looked uneasily at Loz as Gary introduced him as 'Reece.'

Loz vaguely recognised him from school. Reece explained that he had joined the school a few weeks before Gary and was also an out of area boy. He informed Loz that he had moved away from a small village outside of Dartford after his parents had separated.

Loz instantly felt a rapport with Reece and Gary. There was an unseen, unspoken chemistry between them and they each recognised it. The exchange between them promised something new, exciting and fresh and Loz looked forward to new adventures with his new found friends. He kicked himself for not taking the time to befriend the two boys when they had first arrived at his school.

The three boys continued to chat for the remainder of the night until ten thirty approached. The attendees sensed the end of the disco was approaching and the sullenness tried to invade the disco. Loz was in the middle of being educated by Gary on the origins of Hip Hop when the first slow record begun. *'True'* by Spandau Ballet invited couples to dance together. Slowly the dance floor filled with boys and girls from most of the tribes. Mod girls danced with Soul boys, Skinhead boys with Punk girls, New Romantic girls with Mod boys. The sight of embracing bodies dancing awkwardly with each other amused Loz.

Loz noticed Reece nodding his chin indicating that he needed to turn around. Loz got the point and turned to see Theresa standing alone a few feet away from him. Loz suddenly felt nervous and unsure what his next move should be. Theresa waited patiently while Loz fought with himself. Then Gary gently pushed him forward. Loz smiled at Theresa and held his hand out. Theresa accepted it and he led her to a dark area of the dance floor as the first few bars of George Michael's *'Careless Whisper'* begun.

Theresa pulled Loz's body into her as she leaned in to kiss him. Loz clung onto her tightly whilst trying to block out the embarrassment he felt. Loz had always disliked slow dances. Loz and Theresa danced together for the next two slow songs until the music stopped and the main lights were switched on. He pulled himself away from Theresa who had been leaning her head against his chest in between snogging him. Loz glanced around the disco at the other blurry eyed couples. He looked over at Gary and Reece and they gave him the thumbs up before waving their goodbyes. Robert, Neil and the others were all snogging and groping girls whilst the disco organisers were trying to usher the young people out of the church. Theresa gazed lovingly up into Loz's eyes. Loz smiled shyly back, planted a last kiss on her lips then told her that he would phone her as soon as possible. She looked at him longingly then wiggled off in her white stiletto shoes.

THE PLACE I LOVE

'Budge over tubs,' said Loz squashing himself into the seat next to Piggy who he had not seen since the disco after their last day at school. Neil and his brother Paul sat in the seats opposite rolling fags and giggling at a copy of Play boy. Sitting behind him were Robert and Nick discussing West Ham's recent dip in performance whilst Dani and Tina sat in the seats in front flicking through pages of the *Melody Maker*.

There were eighteen bodies crammed into the fourteen seat Howard Wardell's mini bus. Dave the youth club manager drove the mini bus whilst rolling himself fags with one hand and steering the mini bus with the other. It was exactly ten in the morning as Dave reversed the vehicle out of the Howard Wardell car park. The atmosphere in the mini bus was electric with excitement and anticipation. The boys spat insults at each other calling one another names like Joey, Pleb and handjob whilst the girls looked on disapprovingly. As the mini bus turned right at the end of the road Nick, Piggy, Paul and Neil did a moony at Nick's dad who was sweeping up broken glass outside the pub. He smiled as he stuck two fingers up. The mini bus roared down the street to the wild humming from the travellers of the '*Joe 90*' theme tune.

The mini bus was twenty miles up the M20 before those on board calmed down. Loz had exhausted himself five minutes before the others and now gazed out of the window. He had found himself reflecting on the various events of the past few weeks. It felt like a great deal had happened in short space of time. He felt like the changes were coming quick and fast. He pondered on where it was all heading. He couldn't shake off the image of the mannequin in 'Hucks'. Loz caught the reflection of himself in the mini bus mirror. The coat, shirt and jean's that he wore no longer felt like they belonged to him. He felt confused and curious. Loz was content to chew over his thoughts but Robert leaned over the top of the seat and interrupted him.

'Did you see that new boy from school body popping the other night at the Trinity?' he thundered.

'I did, what a load of bollocks.' Neil interjected.

'Too right I thought it looked hilarious,' added Tina.

'You was talking to that boy and his mate for ages Loz. What are they like?' asked Dani.

Loz defended his two new friends.

'They're alright actually. Reece, the one with the big nose comes across a bit shy but that's okay. Then Gary is the tall one. He comes from Yorkshire. Gary was the one doing the body popping.'

Paul looked up from the dirty mag and added the comment that body popping was really catching on and sweeping through the nation like a plague. Loz and the others paid attention to Paul as he informed them that he had been keeping an eye open and announced that the *Breakdance* film was responsible for brain washing the working and middle class youths of Britain into ditching their old clothes and records and adopting the American look instead. Paul completed his summary of the changing times by prophesising that the *Tube* and *Top Of The Pops* would be full to the brim with Hip Hop and electronic drum beats within two years. Loz and the others laughed out loud. Loz was left feeling like Paul's words had heralded the end of the world as they knew it. He was not sure if he was ready for such a dramatic change. Loz was open to a new pair of trainers or a shirt but he was uncertain if he wanted a whole new youth sub-culture. Especially one so heavily rooted in the influences from the United States of America.

Piggy disturbed Loz's considerations by popping open a packet of crisps.

'Here give us one?' said Paul holding out his hand.

'Didn't you have any breakfast' resisted Piggy

'Come on you tight git.'

'Yeah come on fatty,' cried Neil as he snatched the bag of crisps from Piggy. Piggy tried to grab them back but Neil was already stuffing a handful of crisps into his mouth. He then threw the bag to his brother who woofed the remaining crisps down before Piggy could get out of his seat. Piggy hissed a few insults then sunk back into his seat and removed a Chocolate egg from his inside pocket.

'That's green,' said Loz, spying the egg.

Piggy shielded the egg before replying 'Yeah it's a limited edition. Simon stole a load of them from the corner shop on Grecian Street.'

Loz grinned whilst he removed the silver foil wrapping from his orange flavour biscuit that Dave had handed to him as he had stepped onto the mini bus and started to chew off the chocolate from off the edges. He did the same with the chocolate biscuit that followed too. Piggy licked his lips as he watched Loz work on the biscuit. Loz caught him staring at him and slowly began to sing 'If you like a lot of chocolate on your biscuit join our club'. The familiar tune grabbed the attention of the others on the mini bus and within seconds everybody was chanting the same tune. Gradually the harmless words were replaced with 'If you like a lot of aggro with your football join our club'. They sang the tune over and over again whilst Dave pleaded with them to 'SHUT UP'.

The journey into London took over an hour but this was partly due to the traffic jams caused by the Sunday's religious rush hour. Dave cursed the selfish driving habits of others as they passed through New Cross heading towards the Old Kent Road. On their left was an adventure play ground that Loz had once been allowed to play in during a Royal Mail outing that was returning from a performance of *Holiday On Ice*. The men wetted their whistles in the pub opposite whilst the woman kept watch over their children to protect them from the 'coloureds'.

Dave continued to spit curses at the other road users as they drove down the Old Kent Road where Paul and Neil argued over which pub Henry Cooper used to box in. They passed through the Elephant and Castle with lesser obstructions and before long they were racing over the Thames. Dave yelled out that they would be visiting the Petticoat Lane market first and a few minutes later Dave was reversing into a parking spot just a spitting distance from the market. The youth clubbers erupted into a frenzy of collecting their possessions and checking that they had all they needed before descending on the market. Dave shouted to be heard over the chaos trying to introduce the group rules, expectations and where they should meet if anyone got lost. Everybody nodded but didn't really pay attention. Dave knew his requests had been ignored but had no choice so he opened the mini bus doors and unleashed his flock onto the unsuspecting Londoners.

The last thing that Loz heard Dave yelling was something relating to being alert and mindful to pick pockets. Loz's group consisted of himself, Robert, Piggy, Paul and Neil. The five boys weaved their way through the aisles of the market and mingled with the shoppers who carried bags of vegetables and items of clothing.

'Not much has changed really has it?' remarked Paul removing a three quarter length sheepskin coat from a coat rail. Loz noticed they were in fact surrounded by leather and sheepskin coats. The odour was over whelming. The noise in the market place was manic. Shoppers haggled over prices with traders and traders advertised their products with shouts and yells. The smell of hot dogs and burgers wafted through every aisle. Loz liked the atmospheres that market places produced. It was a unique atmosphere.

The boys roamed the market heading in no place in particular. They were all enjoying exploring somewhere new except for Robert who complained that they were wasting their time. Robert was saving his money for their visit to Carnaby Street which is where they were heading for after PettiCoat Lane market. The smell of burgers and hot dogs overcame them so they decided to join the queue at the next hot dog stand that they came across. They each bought a hot dog except Piggy who bought two.

Whilst they bit off large chunks of hot dogs and dripped Ketchup onto themselves Paul spotted Dani and Tina.

'Oi oi!' said Paul, demanding the attention of the other's.

Dani and Tina were sitting on a low wall surrounded by a group of boys. The boys were evidently attempting to 'chat' the girls up and the girls were inviting their advances eagerly. Paul ate his hot dog as quickly as he could whilst taking an instant dislike to the group of boys. Loz had sensed what Paul was thinking and knew what would be coming next.

'Come on' said Paul setting off in the direction of Dani, Tina and the boys. Loz sighed and followed with the others. Paul pushed his way through the group of boys and plonked himself down besides Dani.

'You alright?' he asked.

The two girls nodded and gave him a look which told him to fuck off because they were enjoying themselves. Paul understood but chose to ignore it. He climbed to his feet and looked the London boys up from head to toe. Loz had already been fixated on the London boys clobber. He thought they looked brilliant dressed in their pastel coloured jumpers with Argyle patterns on them, roll necks with Golden Eagle badges on them, bright coloured jumbo cords which were either frayed at the bottom or had splits cut into them. The boys wore either white trainer's with a blue or red tick on them. Their appearance reminded Loz of the mannequin in 'Hucks' again and his new friends Gary and Reece. All the London boys had wedge hair styles.

Paul grunted a few words which Loz didn't hear. He thought the London boys would react but they didn't. One of their gang appeared to assume leadership and calmed his friends down before addressing Paul.

'What's the prob then mate?' he asked tucking his hands into the pockets of his electric blue jumbo cords. The boy spoke calmly in a way that unnerved Loz. Loz felt anxious and suspected that Paul had stirred up something they were all going to regret.

'My problem is you lot chatting up our girls,' Paul hissed.

Dani and Tina tried to protest but Paul turned his back on them. There were four London boys but five visitors. Paul fancied his chances. Paul and the casual's spokesman continued to exchange a few more words and Loz could tell that Paul was losing his patience. The London boy however seemed to be biding his time. This worried Loz. Loz prayed that Dave would appear and diffuse the situation but instead of Dave appearing four more friends of the casuals did. This is why their leader had been stalling. The addition of the four extra London boys now outweighed the visitors.

One of the new additions was a tall black male with a tight afro. He appeared to be a couple of years older than everyone else involved. It looked resplendent the way his black skin complimented his bright yellow track suit top and matching bottoms. He assessed the situation by looking Loz and his friends up and down before walking directly over to Paul and smacking him around the side of the face. Loz heard the hard slap and winced. Paul momentarily lost his balance then returned a punch that missed its target. The black male was about to laugh but Neil stepped forward and swung a punch at him. It connected and the black male looked shocked at first and then angry.

Piggy was the next to get involved. He jumped on the back of one of the boys and it pushed him to the ground. Robert and Loz then launched themselves at the opposition and a fight erupted.

Loz found himself exchanging kicks and punches with another boy wearing a blue roll neck jumper with a Golden Eagle badge on the neck. Loz admired it between the punches. Robert was rolling around on the dirty floor with another boy and Piggy defended himself against an assault of stamps from two mean looking boys with matching rugby jumpers that had Bennt advertised over the chest area.

Loz fell to the floor due to someone grabbing him by the neck from behind. The boy he had been fighting fair and square saw his opportunity and attempted to stamp down onto Loz's head. Loz managed to avoid the stamp and grabbed the boy's foot instead. He then twisted the boy's leg and the boy screamed.

Dani and Tina yelled and screamed in between unleashing the occasional slap on the heads and faces of the London boy's. Market stall traders and shoppers stood by looking disgusted and disapprovingly. The brawl lasted for several minutes before someone pressed an invisible switch and the two armies separated. Each boy stood sweating and panting. The stand-off lasted only a few seconds before another invisible bell chimed indicating round two was upon them. Only this time Loz and his friends ran. Loz ran behind Piggy pushing him forward and Paul led the way through the aisles. The London boys couldn't be bothered and fired insults and threats at the escaping boys instead.

Loz and Robert somehow became separated from the others and ran in amongst the stalls and shoppers until they came across a collection of wooden crates. Robert dived behind them and grabbed Loz by the arm. The two boys fell to the floor sweating and laughing. Loz was already developing a swollen eye and Robert nursed a bloody cut on his cheek.

'Fucking hell!' started Robert 'They were fucking tough.'

'Too fucking right. Mind you they looked good' replied Loz.

The two fell about laughing again.

Loz and Robert nursed their wounds and stocked up on some energy and confidence before creeping back to the mini bus. Dave was trying to give Paul a bollocking but he wasn't paying much attention. The rest of the fighters stood around clutching the wounds on their faces and bodies. They looked a defeated mess. One after the other they climbed aboard the mini bus, found their seats and recounted their personal demonstrations of bravery and toughness. Loz avoided the bravado and stared out of the window instead. He replayed the fight in his mind but only so he could see the clothes the boys were wearing again. Loz had been completely impressed by their look.

Dave drove away from Petticoat Lane market and headed for their next destination which was to be Carnaby Street. They crossed one of the London bridges and then another. It became evident that Dave was lost. His passengers didn't help with their chanting of 'You don't know what you're doing, you don't know what you're doing.'

Eventually Dave got his bearings and fought his way through narrow Soho streets. The boys ogled the prostitutes who stood invitingly in the door ways of their seedy establishments and stuck their middle fingers up at the gays that they passed. Dave even joined in a couple of times. They drove through the same streets a few times passing the infamous jazz club 'Ronnie Scotts' twice. 'There, there,' yelled a few passengers spotting a parking space big enough for the mini bus in Wardour Street and Dave claimed it for his own.

Dave parked the vehicle and turned off the engine but before the passengers could jump out of the mini bus Dave barred their exit.

'Now listen here you lot. I'm being serious. I do NOT want any trouble. Look at yourselves you got mullered back there. You look a mess and I'll be surprised if they let you inside of the shops down there. So be careful and be clever. Keep your wits about you and be back here in one hour. Now sod off'.

Once Loz got off the mini bus he grabbed Robert's arm and asked him if he wanted to stay clear of the others and go exploring by themselves. Robert nodded and they separated themselves from the others. They watched Paul, Neil and Piggy heading off in a different direction shouting at the top of their voices 'Is there an A bomb in Wardour Street?' Loz shook his head.

'I've not been to Carnaby Street before. Have you?' asked Robert.

'Yeah, only a few times though. In fact the last time I visited Carnaby Street was around my birthday last year. I came up with my mum, my aunt and Simon just before his dad got posted to another barracks. I have fond memories of that day actually. It had been a school day but my mum allowed me to have the day off. I think the train fares were cheaper mid-week or something like that. The funniest thing was my mum turning a blind eye to Simon coming with us. It was not planned and I didn't even know he was coming. He simply turned up at mine in the morning clutching a carrier bag. I let him indoors and he stripped off his school uniform and swopped them for jeans and so on. I think my mum and aunt admired his 'front' so said nothing and we went to catch the train. I'll always remember that about my mum.'

'Yeah she's sound your mum mate. So what did you go to Carnaby Street for anyway?'

'I wanted one of them Green army trench coats which at the time was the only place I knew where to get one. Then as a bonus my aunt bought me a target tee-shirt from Sherry's. I was well chuffed.'

'I haven't seen your trench coat' noted Robert.

'No, when I bought it, it was too big but my mum said it could be altered to fit me better. I had it altered on the sleeves but it's still like rent a tent so I stopped wearing it yonks ago' said Loz, and then added 'Even my target tee-shirt has shrunk now too.'

They strolled along Wardour Street, passed through a few alley ways and stepped onto the remaining coloured pavement stones of Carnaby Street. Although Loz was excited about being in Carnaby Street he still felt a degree of sadness for it. He accepted that Carnaby Street had long left behind it's hey days of the heady swinging sixties. Loz loved looking at pictures of the Mod's standing outside Lord John looking cool as fuck. He used to own a poster of The Small Faces flicking through shirts in one of the Carnaby boutiques but he had since lost the poster.

Robert looked more awestruck with the sights and sounds of the Mod's mecca. He marvelled at the rows of fishtail parkas hanging up and the massive selection of Mod friendly tee-shirts. They dipped in and out of shops like Sherry's, Mellandes and Shelly's where they dribbled over the racks of Jam shoes. Loz still desired owning the blue and black bowling shoes one day. He contented himself that he still owned the red, white and blue ones. Robert bought a tee shirt of The Beat. It was red, white and black with the words *'W'happen'* written on it.

Loz left Robert day dreaming in Shelly's window whilst a shop opposite caught his attention. He ambled over to it and his eyes sparkled. The shop window was packed full of casual's clobber. Loz studied the clothes and read the labels to educate himself on the brand names of the items. Loz read names he had not known before. Loz knew he needed to memorise all the names for his future reference and sanity. The casual clothes were rapidly becoming the thing of both his dreams and nightmares.

Robert sided up to Loz and huffed which he followed with the comment. 'It's a bloody insult to Carnaby Street.'

'What do you mean?' asked Loz.

'Well, this is a street for Mod's isn't it? not the casuals.'

'It shows us that times are changing Robert.'

'Not for me they're not' he replied, then spat on the floor and walked away.

They continued to walk down the other side of the street until they stumbled over a narrow doorway. There were steps leading upwards and a sign that advertised a record shop. Robert looked at Loz and nodded his chin in the direction of the door. He then stepped inside and started to walk up the stairs. Loz followed.

At the top of the stairs there was a small landing where three Skinheads sat dressed in their bleached denim jackets and army boots with more lace holes in them than holes in the roads of Blackburn, Lancashire. The skins looked hard and mean but didn't bat an eyelid as Loz and Robert stepped over them to enter the record shop. The room was only small but packed full of boxes containing thousands of records. The owner of the shop sat behind the counter flicking through a wooden box of records. He looked up to get a measure of his new customers then returned to flicking through the record box. Loz started searching through the nearest record box and a moment later Chubby Checkers *'At the discoteque'* started to play.

Loz got a buzz to just be in a record shop in London, let alone Carnaby Street. The buzz got amplified as he realized he was searching through a large box of Northern Soul forty fives. Loz elbowed Robert to show him the collection. Robert's mouth dropped as he too realized he had never encountered so many Northern Soul records in one place at one time. The owner glanced up at the two boys and recognised their fascination.

'These may be of interest to you they only came in yesterday'. And with that he passed them a handful of records. Loz and Robert flicked through the records and both stopped in awe at the same time. Tucked into the middle of the collection was a forty five with an Orange label that had Bandy written on it. Loz grinned at Robert and he grinned back.

'Fucking hell its *Fortune Teller*' whispered Robert.

'I fucking know. Benny 'fucking' Spellman.' Loz replied looking stunned.

Loz looked at the record then at Robert then back at the record. The record had become an anthem at the discos that they had grown up with. One or two of the older Mod's owned copies and they commanded respect because of it. Both boys knew they had to own it. Loz dreaded to know the price but plucked up the courage. He cleared his throat and turned towards the shop keeper. 'How much for this one?'

The owner of the shop looked at the record, then at Loz, then at Robert and then back at the record and said.

'Five pound!'

Loz and Robert sighed as they rummaged in their pockets for the money. They knew that five pounds was a lot of money to them but they knew they would not be leaving the shop without a copy each. They handed over two five pound notes and the shop keeper dropped one copy of the record into a Brown paper bag and handed it to Robert. He then did the same with the second copy and passed it to Loz. Both boys could hardly contain their excitement but did their utter most best to keep their cool as they exited the shop and stepped carefully over the Skinheads on the way out.

Once they were out in the street the two boys set off in the direction of the mini bus beaming at each other. They were so consumed with their conversation relating to their magnificent purchase that they took a wrong turn and found themselves in an unfamiliar street. They walked through a few more streets until they stood outside a pub called the Glasses House.

'Fucking hell' cried Robert as a fat Skinhead came running towards them. The Skinhead had Ox blood boots on, rolled up denim jeans but he had no shirt on. Loz and Robert looked at each other for an answer to their next move. They were about to run off but realized that the Skinhead was not running for them. He was just drunk and running at no one in particular. He looked like a demented Buster Bloodvessel. Loz pushed Robert into the entrance way of the pub just as the fat skin bounced passed them. Loz looked at Robert and laughed.

'Did you read that tattoo on his belly?' asked Loz.

'No, I couldn't make it out, what did it say?'

'Suck it or fuck it and them he had an arrow pointing downwards towards his bollocks.' Loz chuckled.

'Class' said Robert joining in with the laughter.

After making sure the coast was clear from any other fat Skinheads Loz led the way which eventually meant they stumbled on the mini bus. They were the last ones to return. Dave looked pissed off and told them to hurry up and find their seats. Loz and Robert sat next to each other and showed off their copies of *Fortune teller* to the green eyed monsters. The mini bus was full of chatter about their adventures for the entire journey home. Piggy repeatedly yelled 'Nice legs shame about the face' through the window at the girls outside. Dave chained smoked and got lost again but no one cared.

Once Loz got home he hastily shared some of his adventures with his mum and dad who were just being polite because really they were more concerned with watching the snooker. Loz raced up to his bedroom and played his new record ten times straight. He reminded himself of names of the brands on the casual clothes and gazed out of the sky light window. His last thoughts before he drifted off into sleep was

'Today has been a good day'.

ME SHIP CAME IN

'It's Tuesday' yelled Loz's mum up from the bottom of the stairs. Loz woke up abruptly and processed what his mum had said before yelling back.

'So!'

'So, it's the third week of the summer holidays, so get yourself down the dole office or job office. TODAY.'

'Yeah, yeah.' Loz mumbled.

'Just make sure you do. Besides its signing on day today so you'll probably bump into all your mates' she added sarcastically.

Her last words faded which meant Loz's mum had retreated to the kitchen. Loz scratched his balls and then the few bristles appearing on his chin. As he eased himself out of his pit he caught a wiff of his own body odour. He winced and shook his head. Loz puffed his cheeks out and blew out the air slowly. He coughed as he remembered some of the events of the previous night.

Loz's dad had decided it would be good for the family to go for a quiet drink up the Civil Service club. Loz's dad said he would drive for a change even though they only lived a few streets away. His dad owned a dark green Vauxhall Viva. Loz had no plans so didn't resist and challenged his dad to game of pool. However once they arrived at the club it turned out that there was a party for one of the Prison Officers that were celebrating his pending retirement.

Loz and his family found a table in the members bar area away from the party. Loz's dad ordered a pint of beer in a jug. He only ever drank his beers out of jugs and not straight glasses. Loz was allowed a half pint of lager but he had to keep it out of sight. His brother got a fizzy drink and his sister a spirit with Lemonade whilst Loz's mum got a medium glass of red wine.

The family enjoyed one another's company. Loz and his dad played several games of pool before his dad slipped away to play on the fruit machines. As the night wore on Loz noticed that his dad was getting more and more pissed. He thought about reminding him that he was driving but forgot to mention it.

The bell for last orders rang at ten minutes to eleven. Loz's dad gathered the family up and ushered them to their car. They all got inside and Loz's dad drove them home. It was only when they pulled up outside their house that Loz's brother asked why there was a toddler's toy on the floor underneath his feet. Loz's sister picked up the toy and waved it in the air. Everybody looked at it confusingly. Then Loz's mum spotted a packet of Rothmans cigarettes on the dash board. Only then did it dawn on her that it was not there car. Loz's dad realized what he had done and spun the car around. He drove back to the Civil service club to find a man looking bemused and standing beside another green Vauxhall Viva in the car park.

Loz's dad got out of the car first and had a conversation with the man. A few seconds later the two men were laughing together. It turned out that Loz's dad's car keys also fitted the other man's Viva and in his slightly pissed state had not noticed he had ushered the family into the wrong car.

Loz continued to chuckle to himself as he stretched and yawned. He was in need of some gentle sounds to wake up to. Normally he was not a slow burner in the mornings but today his body felt a little tired. Loz chose The Questions 'Building on a strong foundation'. He slipped on a grey sweat shirt and a pair of jeans and dragged himself down stairs to the kitchen.

By the time he reached the kitchen his mum had already left for work. Loz toasted some bread and covered it in butter and crab paste which he then washed down with two cups of sweet tea. Following this he combed his hair, put on his deck shoes and set off in the direction of town.

At the bottom of the street a few young children were playing marbles on the embossed lines of the drain cover outside of the corner shop. Loz remembered playing exactly the same game when he was their age. Loz also remembered being sent to the corner shop which, like all corner shops opened every day from nine to seven except for Wednesdays which was half day opening. Loz recalled the shelves of the shop being stacked with only a few items. There would be bags of tea, sugar and coffee which the old shop keeper would remove from the shelf and weigh out what you required on even older metal scales before tipping the goods into another paper bag.

Loz peered into the corner shop thinking it looked like it was on its last legs. The shop keeper looked tired and so did the old corner shop. As Loz crossed the road and walked in the shadow of the prison wall he felt sad for the corner shops. In the last couple of years Loz had noticed that some of the corner shops and traditional old pubs that surrounded him and occupied most street corners were slowly closing down and turning into apartments, video hire or double glazing shops. Loz considered the pubs and corner shops to be the back bone of his community. They were the arteries through which every bit of gossip travelled. They supplied the kids with gob stoppers, mums with their groceries and dads with their pints. Loz prayed that this would always stay the same, but deep down he knew it wouldn't.

To lift his mood he pondered on the football casuals clothes that he had seen at the Petticoat Lane market and in the shop window on Carnaby Street. Loz found himself dwelling on the London boys wedge hairstyles. He wondered what he would look like if he had his hair styled the same way. He was still trying to picture himself with a wedge when he found himself standing at the entrance to Barny's the hairdressers. He had plenty of time to kill so decided to pop into Barny's to have a chat with Sweeny Mod who worked in the hairdressers.

Loz had been going to Barny to get his hair cut for a couple of years. He had spent most of his growing up years getting dragged to the hairdressers near his house but they didn't know what a French line was and so by the time Loz was thirteen his mum allowed him to go to Barny's. At first she escorted him but gradually she began to trust him and let him go by himself. Loz's mum knew her son was too sensible to return home one day with a grade one skinhead or even worse, bleached highlights.

Since Loz had been going to Barny's Barny had employed a hip and trendy young man who was himself a Mod. His real name was Dave but all the Mod's that went to him for the Mod haircuts nicknamed him Sweeny Mod.

Loz climbed the stairs that led into the hair dressers shop. Along one side of the room was a row of seats and mirrors. There were several shelves with hair dryers, scissors and hand mirrors stacked neatly. On the other side of the room there was one basin used for washing people's hair in. *'Dig the new breed'* was being played on a portable stereo at the far end of the shop.

The owner Barny was busy snipping away and chatting to a customer, it was a soul boy with highlights in his hair. Sweeny Mod was lounging across a leather sofa that the customers used when they were waiting to be seen. Sweeny Mod was looking very sharp and Italian in his polished loafers, turned up white jeans and blue and white breton strip tee-shirt.

'Alright Sweeny, you're looking dapper mate' said Loz.

'Hello Loz, you know me I'm keeping up to speed. You know I saw this brilliant picture of Weller the other day. He was walking along the road in his latest Style Council togs right. I mean beige trench coat, turn ups on his trousers, tasselled loafers and slick back hair. And then watching him were a group of young Mod's. I'm talking thirteen and fourteen year olds. Only they were clad in Parkas, desert boots and bowling shoes. You see Weller has moved far away from that it's just that it hasn't filtered down to the masses. That's why Weller is a proper Mod. He is always moving on and fucking miles in front of everyone else. Anyway Loz what can I do you for?'

'Well Sweeny it's a bit along those lines you're jabbering on about really. I'm looking for a bit of advice.'

'Oh yeah, fire away then mate.' Sweeny sunk deep into the sofa.

'What do make of those wedge haircuts that all the footy casuals are sporting then?'

Sweeny Mod appeared to be surprised with the question and sniffed a few times before answering.

'Well the wedge goes with the look don't it in the same way a grade one goes with a pair of Ox blood boots, a French line goes with a Mohair jacket with three buttons and long greasy hair goes with Patchouli oil. You see the casuals hairstyles vary depending on where you're from and what team you support. For example up Liverpool it's all perms and moustaches, where as in Manchester it's the Mullet and other places the wedge. Why? What's your interest? You thinking of turning into a casual then?'

Loz perched himself on the edge of the sofa and glanced over at Barny who was running his boney fingers through the soul boy's freshly cut hair.

'Yeah, I'm interested Sweeny. I like the look, the clothes, the attitude. The whole thing feels really fresh and new.'

'New for you and the general public Loz but the casual thing has been going on for years up north. Only up there they dressed like sailors and shepherds' he laughed.

'I mean it's just the look aint it. It's nothing to do with music.'

'It's all about football Loz. Whilst one footy team is trying to outdo the other team on the pitch their fans are trying to outdo the other team's fans on the terraces either in a battle or in fashion.'

This had not occurred to Loz before and he liked Sweeny Mods perception.

'So yeah I am interested in the clothes but I can still like and listen to the same music as always can't I?'

'Yeah of course. Look, some of that casual gear is okay and in truth some of it is very Mod like with the style of tee shirts, but, it's not my cup of tea, I'm a Mod and I'll die a Mod. You know what they say 'Once a Mod, always a Mod'. So does that help Loz?'

Loz nodded and looked into space before asking. 'So what do I need to do to grow a wedge then? If that's what I decided to do at some point.'

Sweeny Mod assessed Loz's current hair style before telling him that he would need to let it grow for a few more weeks and then come back to the shop to see him. Just then a fresh customer entered the shop and Sweeny Mod leapt up to greet them. Loz thanked Sweeny Mod for his time and made to leave. Just as he put his foot on the top stair Sweeny Mod called after him.

'I'll see you in a few weeks then dressed in a kagool and a pair of blue boots shall I? And with that he winked.

The walk to the job centre was only ten minutes. Loz took his time. Whilst Loz had been inside Barny's there had been a brief rain shower. Loz breathed in the unique smell that the rain left on pavements on hot, dry days. The town was busy with shoppers and crowds of loitering youths with nothing better to do. Loz reached the High Street and crossed over it avoiding the buses. He then walked down the streets with its banks, over the bridge that crossed the river Medway and strolled up the hill to the Job centre.

The job centre was located in an old grey stone building that looked like it may have been a court house at one time. A massive orange and white sign hung over the doorway advertising it was the Job centre. Loz felt slightly ashamed as he entered the building. He looked left and then right at the notice boards with their small cards on them. Loz noticed that there were more empty gaps than there were cards. Loz walked over the nearest notice board and read the dozen small cards that advertised what jobs were available. Loz read the first one. It was for a factory workers post in a meat packing factory. The second was a shelf stacker in Tesco's and the third a fruit picker.

Loz sighed and scanned the room. His mum had been correct, the Job Centre was busy with men and woman of all ages reading the small cards and standing in the queue that led them to their dole cheques. Loz decided against joining the queue and exited the Job Centre. He told himself that he needed a cup of tea so headed off in the direction of the Wander Inn.

The Wander Inn was hot and packed full with customers chomping on their bacon butties. Tuesdays was not only Job Centre day but also market day. This meant the town was ten times busier than normal. Sometimes Loz would venture down the market. There was the main part of the market that sold groceries, clothes and other house hold goods, but in the old sheep shed was a boot sale. Loz's dad would make a bee line for the boot fair whilst his mum bought the groceries and other things the family actually needed. Loz occasionally discovered a gem in the boot sale, a record or an old football programme. The boot sale area was more relaxed too, away from the yelling market traders and Loz preferred this.

Loz waited in the queue until it was his turn to order a cup of tea. The coffee machines gurgled and the frying pans hissed. He felt hungry but he didn't have enough cash to buy any food. Instead he carefully balanced his cup of hot steaming tea on its saucer and found himself a seat. On the table in front of him a toddler was ravishing a cream donut. The child had cream, jam and sugar all over his face. The child's mother puffed away on a fag and sipped her tea.

The sight of the cream donut triggered a memory in Loz. It was the same memory he always got when he saw a cream donut. When he was eleven years old Loz and his next door neighbour were allowed to go the pictures by themselves to watch Star Wars. Before they entered the cinema they bought a cream donut each from the bakers opposite the cinema. It was a tradition that had begun a few years earlier whenever Loz or his friends were taken to the cinema they were always given cream donut's to munch on whilst they waited in the long cinema queue's. That day Loz and his neighbour watched Star Wars was special though. For some reason they had arrived late and the film had already begun. However at the end of the film the usherette sided up them and told them that because they missed the start of the film they could stay put and watch the entire film again. The two young boys were made up and accepted the offer. So, they got to watch Star Wars twice in one day.

The toddler starred at Loz as he drunk his tea. Loz starred back at him and the child smiled revealing his dimples. In turn, this made Loz smile. Loz did not notice the café door swing open and two Skinheads walk in. Loz lowered his head to avoid being seen. It was unusual for the Skinheads to use the Wander Inn. They used a café in Littlewoods and normally steered away from the Mod's Wander Inn. Loz watched them in their green flight jackets join the queue. As soon as they were being served Loz slipped past them unnoticed and bolted up the street. He wondered if the

81

Skinheads were looking for him or the others involved in the fight with Webby. Loz had not thought about the fight for a couple of weeks. He assumed it had blown over and Webby no longer cared for revenge. Loz hoped he wasn't wrong.

Loz ran out of places to go and money so headed home. He found his brother sitting in front of the television gawping over an episode of *Grange Hill*. Loz's mum was in the kitchen baking scones. The kitchen smelt great due the first batch of hot scones sitting on a baking tray. Loz helped himself to a scone, cut it in half and scooped up a large amount of butter and spread it on both sides. It instantly melted and Loz took a bite. It tasted delicious and familiar. It pleased him that his mum liked baking.

Loz's mum quizzed him over his visit to the Job Centre. Loz made himself a cup of tea whilst he fabricated a story that included something to do with a new initiative available known as the YTS or Youth Training Scheme. Loz's mum looked at him suspiciously. Loz filled his mug with water and watched the water turn a dirty brown colour.

'Why don't you ever fill the mug to the top?' asked his mum.

'I don't know, habit I 'spose. I always leave a drop at the bottom too.' He replied.

His mum shook her head then probed further about this new youth scheme.

'So what does the scheme involve?'

'The one I enquired about was a trainee car paint sprayer and panel beater up at Dutton's.'

'But you don't like cars and mechanical things,' She said

'I know, but I like paint.'

'You do know it's not going to be painting model aeroplanes with those tiny paints don't you?'

Loz thought about the wonderful smell of the air fix paints and the hours he had spent as younger child carefully painting his soldiers and models with the paints.

'Yes I know. I'll have to be interviewed first anyway. The pay is not great though, it's only twenty seven pounds and fifty pence.'

'Jesus, is that all' She huffed then got distracted with the removal of more scones from the oven. Loz saw his opportunity to escape further questions. He snatched another scone and legged it up to his bed room.

Loz had an hour to kill before he needed to be heading out again. He had arranged to meet his friend John around the Howard Wardell. Loz had also promised John a compilation tape of Northern Soul tunes. Loz stripped down to his boxer's and picked various soul records from his tape collection. He plugged in the tape cassette that he had owned since he was a small boy and un-wrapped a C60 tape cassette which he then shoved into the tape machine.

Compiling music tapes for friends was one of Loz's favourite things to do. He was generous in that way and had probably compiled hundreds. There was something about sharing his musical taste and 'turning' others on to new sounds that Loz liked. It was also his way of expressing himself and identifying who he was. Over the years he had compiled tapes of Soul, Ska, Reggae and a whole host of bands from the first and second generation of Mod.

'*Move on up*' by Curtis Mayfield kicked off the recording session. Loz loved The Jam's live version but the original made the hairs on the back of his neck stand up every time. The next track was '*Queen of fools*', the next '*Come on train*' which Loz had originally copied from his red vinyl Inferno album. Following this he included '*Tainted Love*', '*Compared to what*', '*Out on the floor*', '*Fortune teller*' and '*The Night*'.

The hour raced by but Loz had just enough time to record the final record '*Landslide*' before rushing out of the house and heading off to meet John. His mum was watching *The Price Is Right* on the television as he waved her good night. His dad was flicking through a book on the history of ancient Egypt.

There was a congregation of Loz's friends at the alley way near the Howard Wardell. Some sat on the grass outside the block of flats and some stood chatting inbetween swigs of a cider bottle. Loz walked directly up to his friend John and pushed the tape cassette into the breast pocket on his denim jacket.

'Nice one Loz, smart' thanked John.

'No probs. There's a few rarer tunes mixed in with the classics. They are all good tunes though, and I wrote the songs and artist on the inside.'

'Cheers' said John tapping his breast pocket with a wink.

'Are you staying for the evening?' Loz asked.

'No prob not, I was thinking of going to the hut. Steve and Jason are down there and they will have whisky.'

'Yeah, alright. Say hello to them for me. I aint seen them for a couple of weeks, they don't come up here much anymore.'

Suddenly Loz felt a pair of hands grab him around the neck and swing him around.

'For fuck's sake' cried Loz steadying himself.

'Alright' slurred Paul releasing his grip.

Paul staggered and Loz could smell his stale cider breath. Paul was with a couple of his friends from school whose names were Carl and Lee. They were drunk.

'Give us a fag' Carl demanded.

'I don't smoke' replied Loz.

Carl walked off to hassle someone else for a fag. Lee then offered Loz the bottle of Cider that he was clutching. Loz shook his head which Carl spotted and followed by chanting '*Don't drink don't smoke, what do you do*'. He sung it a couple times before Paul and Lee joined in. Loz shook his head again and made to walk off. Paul playfully jumped onto his back which pushed Loz to the floor. Next, Carl and Lee dived on top of them and the four boys rolled around in the grass. Loz tried to escape but they kept pulling him back to the floor. When he did eventually free himself he yelled out a loud 'FUCKING HELL'. There were grass stains over the knees of his white Jean's.

Loz was livid and spat insults at Paul and his cronies. He knew his jeans were ruined. John sided up to him with words of encouragement trying to assure him that mums can do wonders with washing machines. Loz thanked John but knew his mum would be throwing the jeans in the bin.

The drunks were getting drunker and more irritating so Loz decided to remove himself from their company and he sneaked away. Half way along the alley he could hear the drunks teasing John by singing 'Hello John got a new motor, hello John got a new motor, hello John got a new motor'.

Dave the club manager looked up from his newspaper to accept Loz's twenty pence. The back cover of the newspaper had a photograph of Daley Thompson and Sebastian Coe on it and announced their achievements in the Los Angeles summer Olympics. Loz turned left and walked towards the pool table. He stood arms folded watching his brother and his brothers friend playing. Something from Level 42 was playing on the jukebox. Loz then noticed Theresa sitting by herself on the sofa near the tuck shop. He walked over to her and sat on the arm of the sofa.

Loz thought Theresa looked nice in the blouse she was wearing with a zig zag pattern on it. The blouse was tight and clung to her breast's which drew attention to them. She was also sucking a lollipop which Loz watched her tongue work on. Her lips glistened with the moisture and Loz felt a tremble in his bollocks.

'What happened to you?' she asked noticing the grass stains.

'Bloody Paul and his drunken mate's mucking about.'

'You know you'll never get those stains out don't you?' She said pointing out the obvious and pouting her lips.

'So I'm told. What you been up to then?' He enquired sliding down the sofa so he sat closer to her. His knee touched hers and it excited him.

'I've got a job' she announced 'I applied for half a dozen jobs weeks ago but only got two responses. I start next Monday at the vet's down Boxley Road.'

'What as a vet?' said Loz sounding surprised.

'No you Joey, as a receptionist. Monday to Friday, nine to five which means my evenings will stay free.' She licked her lips.

'Right, okay, that means you can take me out with your first wage packet.'

'You're on,' she replied and she beamed him a smile.

They continued to chat for the next twenty minutes without anybody disturbing them. Loz filled her in on the events of Petticoat Lane market and Carnaby Street. Theresa enquired how his own job hunting was progressing and he lied telling her that he had some offers in the pipeline. Loz bought a dozen half penny sweets and they shared them out then laughed at each other's Blackened tongues. Loz and Theresa were about to kiss but were interrupted by the yells of Nip who came bounding into the room.

'Loz, Loz' He begun whilst trying to catch his breath 'Its Neil, he is outside and he has taken a right pasting'.

'Bollocks. Who from?' said Loz dreading the answer.

'Webby and his mates,' shouted Nip.

Neil was sitting on a low wall leaning forward with his hands over his head. Several youths crowded around him. Amongst them were Paul and his two friends Carl and Lee. Paul looked angry and distraught at the sight of his bloodied younger brother. Various people were firing questions at Neil which he was trying to ignore and answer at the same time. Loz crouched down low beside Neil and looked at him. Neil looked like he was in a state of shock and would burst into tears at any moment. 'Come with me' said Loz and led Neil away from the crowd. Paul followed.

'What the fuck has happened mate?'

Neil cleared his throat and wiped his eyes. 'It was Webby's lot. I was making my way here when they drove past me in their Cortina. I watched them drive up the road a bit and then they spun the car around and drove back to me. Before I knew it Simmons and Roy had grabbed me and dragged me into the car. Next thing they do is pummel the shit out of me. They drove around for a bit until they pushed me out of the car down Wheeler Street.'

Tears began to fall from Neil's eyes as he revisited the ordeal. He had several cuts and bruises on his face and his shirt's collar was torn. Nip and some of the others had re-joined them now and fired more questions at Neil.

'Right, come on' screamed Paul 'Let's find the bastards.'

'They're driving and could be anywhere' someone added.

'Let's try the Wheelers first, they often get in there.' Nick interjected.

Paul led the way and half of the youth club followed. Theresa and Loz held hands walking at the rear whilst Paul marched his troops forward. On route they passed a skip full of discarded builder's materials. Carl, Lee and Paul picked out lumps of wood and a few broken bricks. Loz could see that the older boys were becoming especially pumped up. They marched at pace passing the Dog and Gun, The Holly Bush and the Brickmakers. At each pub Paul poked his nose through the door to see if any of the Skinheads were there.

They continued down the hill turned left and immediately spotted the Skinheads Cortina parked outside the Wheelers. Paul placed his finger over his lips gesturing to his troops to keep quiet whilst he sneaked up to the pub. He peeked through the window and saw the gang of Skinheads playing pool at the rear of the pub.

'This will get their attention' He snarled before running full speed towards the Cortina and smashing his wooden lump onto the window screen. It cracked but didn't shatter. The rest of his army raced towards the car and helped with the destruction of it. Youths kicked, punched and smashed whatever they could lay their hands on over the vehicle. The rear and side windows shattered easily and then door panels caved in under the frenzied attack. Even Theresa smashed her fist down onto the bonnet leaving a few dents in it. The yells, screams and sound of smashing glass alerted the Skinheads and they poured out of the pub.

The car attackers dispersed in all directions in an attempt to evade the angry looking skins. Loz grabbed hold of Theresa's hand and they sped off as fast as their legs would carry them. They ran through a narrow path, pass some cottages and along an alley way beside an allotment. They only paused to catch their breath when they reached the builders merchants and were certain they had outwitted their rivals.

Loz planted a big kiss on Theresa's lips and she pulled him in close to her. They snogged and kissed all the way to the hut where they decided the others would also retreat to, those that had survived the Skinheads anyway.

To their astonishment no one else was at the hut. Loz guided Theresa towards the huts wooden steps where they plonked themselves down. They both felt excited and exhausted. The full moon was just taking shape as the nights sky absorbed the remaining day light. Loz and Theresa sat in silence waiting for the others.

'Fucking hell' started Loz 'That was like the scene from *Quadrophenia* where Jimmy smashes up the drug pushers Jag.'

Theresa just stared back at him and then kissed him. They held each other and snogged. Theresa took hold of Loz's hand and guided it towards her breast. He squeezed and rubbed her. She moaned then pulled the zipper down on his jeans. Loz shuffled so that she could access him easier. Theresa then slid her cold hand down into his pants. Loz manoeuvred his hand inside of her bra. Theresa pushed Loz onto the ground and pulled down his pants and trousers before positioning herself on top of him.

'Have you got a johnny?' she whispered in his ear.

Loz rifled in his jacket pocket and removed a slim rectangle plastic shaped object. He handed it to Theresa who tore one of the ends of it off and spat the bit onto the floor. Loz watched on eagerly as she 'bagged' him in the stinky piece of pink rubber. Even through the rubber the sensation still felt good. They found their rhythm quickly and rocked back and forth. Theresa placed her hands onto his stomach and dug her nails into his skin each time she rocked forwards. Loz stared at her face. She had her eyes closed and looked to Loz like she was having the time of her life.

Theresa moaned and groaned and made noises that Loz had never heard before. Her rocking got faster and faster. Throughout the sighing Theresa smiled down at Loz. She knew she had done a good job. She slid off of him and fumbled around with her knickers. Loz pulled off the Johnny and checked that it was still intact. He sighed again once he was certain it had not split.

Loz threw the used Johnny as far away as he could and started to pull up his trousers when he heard the faint sound of conversation. Theresa heard it to and scampered to her feet whilst sorting her knickers out at the same time. Loz soon followed and straining his eyes could just make out the silhouettes of a few people walking in their direction. He hoped they were his friends and not the skins. Only when the voices got much nearer did Loz recognise them as being Pauls and Neil's.

'Fucking hell that was close' Loz whispered to his lover.

'Too right, if they had caught us you would have got teased with more than just a gobble gobble.'

Loz chuckled then squeezed her hand. Before Paul and Neil got closer they shouted out 'Who's there?'

'Me and Theresa. Where are the others?' replied Loz.

'Fuck knows.' Said Paul, 'We ran towards Watermans. At first we were being chased by Webby and Simmons but we managed to out run them. I remember seeing Nip being chased by Walshy but I don't know if he got away or not' said Paul.

'We did a fucking good job on the bastards motor didn't we?' added Neil.

Theresa pitched in 'Yeah we did but there's gonna be hell to pay now.'

They all knew it but in that moment it all felt worthwhile. They then sat on the wooden steps of the hut and hoped that some of the others would also show up.

'Anyway how long have you two been here and what have you been up to?' asked Neil.

Loz and Theresa didn't reply.

IN THE CROWD

The group of older Mod's vigorously chanted a Jam song as the train pulled away from Bromley south. Loz sat squeezed between Den and one of his friends Gus. Gus was a tall slim male with an Italian complexion who looked the spitting image of Robert De Niro. Gus looked slick in a red buttoned down shirt, Grey, Purple and Red tonic trousers and Brown suede loafers. He had a laid back presence about him that Loz felt comfortable being around. Throughout the train journey Gus had joked and teased anyone and everyone and constantly made references to Bruce Lee.

Two older Mod's, Mark and Malc sat opposite them. Malc was crushing a beer can dressed in his beige Harrington, jeans and Monkey boots. Mark wore a denim jacket and sky blue Levi sta-prest. He had spent the entire journey looking pensive and constantly checking his watch. Their carriage stunk of aftershave and cigarettes. Loz enjoyed listening to their conversations and being the brunt of their sense of humour. The group touched on all manner of topics like music, clothes, girls, scooters and Chelsea football club which was where they were heading.

Malc sunk more cans of beer than anyone else and made them all laugh with his story of pissing against the counter of the Chinese takeaway the previous night whilst being in a drunken state. Gus made them laugh further by recounting the story of the time Malc slept over at his bed sit and pissed himself in the night all over his brand new pull out sofa bed. Loz was fascinated by the chemistry that the two friends had. It was hilarious to watch. They really were as thick as thieves. Mark produced a pack of cards and said they had just enough a time for a quick gamble. Loz and Den declined whilst the other three amused themselves.

'Nice one for bringing me up with you' said Loz.

'No worries mate. It was only after I spoke to Baz that I found out that you were a Chelsea boy. Have you been to the Bridge before?'

'No, never and I don't mind saying that I'm really fucking excited about it.'

'You'll love it but keep your wits about you won't you there's a lot of hard nuts about.'

'You mean the Chelsea Skinheads?' asked Loz.

'No, you'll be alright coz you'll be in the Shed end with them. It's the away fans. Luton will fancy themselves for a while but will soon shit themselves when they feel a size ten boot up their arses.'

Loz laughed and tried to picture the scene of the Luton boys running away. Loz's interest in Chelsea had begun around the time he started listening to The Jam. Somewhere along the line he thought he read that Paul Weller was a Chelsea supporter and because of this decided to do the same. Loz was not certain if that information was correct but it didn't matter any longer he had made his own connection with the club. During the last few years of school Liverpool, Arsenal and West Ham dominated the playground so Loz felt pleased with his choice to set himself apart and support 'The Blues'.

Loz had hardly slept the night before. He was too excited about his first visit to Chelsea's home ground Stamford Bridge. He had waited for the day for so long. He felt excited, nervous and scared. Loz had often read articles in his dad's newspapers about the notorious Chelsea boot boys and Chelsea Skinheads and a newer term Chelsea hooligans. Loz was fascinated with the clubs history and the fans, especially the fans of the nineteen seventies with their boots, donkey jackets and blue and white scarves wrapped around their wrists. Loz wondered what sights he would encounter on his first visit.

'But will there be many Skinheads?' Loz asked again.

'Yeah loads, but they are fading away. When I first started to come up to the Bridge with my uncle all the Skinheads had to remove the laces from their boots and hang them on the fence on the way in'. Den chuckled at his recollection.

'Are we standing in the Shed?'

'Yeah of course. It's the only place to be every other Saturday. It's where all the top boys go too and it's the most vocal area of the ground.'

'So the atmosphere will be good?'

'It will be brilliant Loz. It's the first home game of the season to so there will be a great buzz around. Look you're going to love it,' Den rubbed his hands together excitedly 'And I'll look after you' he added.

Loz needed to hear that. Den then cracked open another can of beer took a large gulp of it before passing it to Loz who also took a swig. Malc was winning the card game and humming *Strange town'*. Malc, Mark and Gus were also arguing over various television programmes.

'Bollocks,' shouted Gus.

'Yeah, you're still mourning the loss of the *Young Ones'* joked Mark.

'No seriously I think that Crocket is a cool looking bloke,' returned Gus.

'Bollocks,' replied Mark.

'Fuck off, you don't know coz you don't watch *Miami Vice* do you?'

'It's American, tasteless shit, that's all I need to know' argued Mark.

'It's not I'm telling you. The stories are good.'

'But you wasn't talking about the stories you was saying that Crocket is a cool dresser. I'm saying all that rolling your sleeves up on your suit jacket is bollocks.'

The last comment silenced Gus, he knew Mark had a point.

'Come on get sorted we are here.' Den announced whilst lighting another fag. Loz stretched his neck to see out of the window. A big sign said 'Victoria Station'. Loz rubbed his hands together excitedly. The carriage got noisy as passengers rustled bags, grabbed their coats and stepped on empty beer cans. Den led the way off of the train and along the platform. He reminded Loz to keep his wits about him because 'Victoria Station' would be full of travelling football fans from Spurs, Palace and Charlton.

As they passed through the barriers Loz saw several groupings of males who were evidently going to football. The older males wore a mixture of donkey jackets, leather jackets and flight jackets whilst the majority of younger males wore casual gear. As Den navigated the way through the crowds he would whisper into Loz's ear what teams the various grouping supported. Loz admired that skill that seasoned footy fans acquire of identifying what teams are being supported. He had been told that footy fans have their individual aura about them. West Ham felt different to Arsenal or Spurs and so on and it was not just the clothes that set them apart. Loz hoped that one day he would obtain that special detective gift.

Loz stuck close to Den as they walked down the steps into the underground station. It was busy and Loz noticed that Den looked worried when he spotted a group of around a dozen boys standing near the entrance to the Central Line.

'Stick close'. Den mumbled to Loz 'That's the top boy from the ICF'.

'Yeah, alright. What's the ICF?'

'Inter-city firm. They are West Ham's mob. Each firm has a name. You have heard of the Chelsea Headhunters aint you? Well other names are the F.E.C Forest executive crew or M.I.G Men in gear. You'll see them today coz they're Luton's firm and fancy themselves as a bunch of switched on dressers, which of course is bollocks.'

Loz was fascinated and wanted to ask more questions about football's hooligan element but he could see that Den was concerned about the loitering I.C.F, plus he didn't want to make himself out to be a complete footy virgin. Loz gave the I.C.F one last discreet glance and wondered what they had in store for some poor defenceless Yids. Loz read the maps of the underground and noticed that Den was leading them in the direction of the Earls Court.

'Where are we going Den?' Loz asked.

'We are taking a short detour to Shepherds Bush. Don't worry I'll still get you to the match for kick off'. He answered with a sparkle in his eye.

Loz felt a mixture of curiosity and anxiety because no one had mentioned a detour to Shepherds Bush. He feared they were going to put him through some kind of initiation or test where they would abandon him and leave him to find his own way to Chelsea whilst having to avoid Yids and Hammers. Then Loz got really scared suspecting he was being led to his first hooligan encounter. He didn't feel ready for a street battle with much older and tougher footy hooligans.

Den sensed Loz's anxiety so reassured him that everything was alright and that he and the others were only popping into a clothes shop in Shepherds Bush. Suddenly the penny dropped and Loz realized the shop must be the one he had read about in the article about Kinnocks son, the shop must be Simons.

'Fucking hell, are we going to Simons?' cried Loz.

'That's right, nice one I'm impressed' replied Den.

'But it's where the casuals shop aint it?'

'Yep, we want to go and check out what they have to sell. It was Mark's idea originally and we have been waiting for the start of the footy season to come up and visit the shop on our way to the game.'

The tube arrived and they stepped onto it. It was hot and devoid of any fresh air. It was also busy with bored and pissed off looking people. Loz plonked himself on a seat opposite a business man in an expensive pin stripe suit and polished brogues who looked at Loz, frowned and turned away. Malc broke into song again and swayed to and fro. Gus and Mark found empty seats further down the carriage and attempted to chat up a posh looking bird who would not have looked out of place on Crockets arm. She huffed, pouted her lips and stepped off the tube at Sloan Square.

The tube ride only lasted ten minutes passing through South Kensington and then Earls Court where they got off. Malc got off first and marched down the platform. There was an old feel about Earls Court with its signs and notice boards that had not been replaced since the nineteen forties. Loz could almost picture the magnificent steam trains with their wooden doors and passengers in their D-mob suits.

Malc continued to lead the way to the platform where they would need to catch the tube to Shepherds Bush. Earls Court was busy with travelling footy fans swapping trains and staring out opposing fans. Nothing was going to happen though due the presence of the tall, serious and tough looking Metropolitan Police officers who relished the thought of battering any hooligans who stepped out of line on their shift.

The tube arrived in just over three minutes and they boarded it. It was another stuffy hot train and somebody had been sick on one of the seats. It stank and made Loz retch. Mark proceeded to open every window and they huddled around them trying to breath in as much fresh air as possible. From Earls Court they passed through Notting Hill Gate before eventually pulling into Shepherds Bush. As the train slowed Malc opened the door and jumped out gasping for air. Loz and the others followed suit.

The five of them walked arrogantly in a row down the platform then up the steps leading out of the tube station. Coming down the steps were several casuals dressed resplendently in brightly coloured track suits and White trainers. A few of them had newspapers stuffed in their back pockets or held them like truncheons. This enhanced their image. They smirked at the Mod's as they passed them. Loz wondered how Den and the others would react. They looked on in awe.

On entering the street outside the station the bright sunlight blinded them. There were rows of red buses and black taxis darting around with passengers getting on and off of them. Immediately outside the station was a newspaper vendor. Mark, Den and Gus bought copies of *The Sun* and stuffed them in their back pockets. They then crossed the busy road in a row emulating the *Abbey Road* album cover. Loz walked at the back and almost had his heels clipped by a black cab. He quickened his pace to catch up with Den.

They strolled down the road in the direction of Simons. Several more boys passed them dressed to the nines in their best sportswear and clutching plastic bags with Simons written on it in big bold letters. It was simple but effective advertising. Loz was the first to see the shop. Outside the shop groups of casuals gathered. They looked tough and intimidating and looked the Mod's up and down as they entered the shop.

The inside of the shop was small and packed full of clothes from wall to wall and ceiling to floor. Loz was instantly impressed by the large collection and variety that the shop offered. It was the most colourful shop Loz had ever seen. His companions appeared equally in awe and dispersed in all directions making a bee line for whatever garment had caught their eye. Loz followed Den who pounced on a rack of jumbo Lois cords. He impatiently searched through them until he found his size. He asked Loz to hold them for him whilst he next checked out some faded jeans. Den gawped at the jeans but screwed his nose up at the price of them before replacing them. Loz then followed him as he moved along to a rack of track suit tops. Den fingered his way through them and Loz looked on taking note of the names on the labels. They were made of every colour under the sun.

Den stopped at a track suit top made of velour. He pulled it out to study it better. It looked fabulous in green and cream with its red, white and blue badge on the chest. He then asked Loz to hold it along with the electric blue Lois cords. They moved along to the next shelves and Den pulled out a green and white Beneton rugby sweatshirt. Den had a massive grin on his face and his eyes were big and wide.

The inside of the shop was busy with young males pushing past and reaching over one another to pick up garments of clothing. The buzz and excitement that filled the air refreshed Loz's belief that something new was a foot and he wanted to be included in it. Den dragged Loz to the counter and Loz plonked the clothes on it. One of the shop keepers with a wedge and moustache took command. Gus and the others were at the other end of the counter also paying for their purchases. They all sported massive grins and the shop keepers filled the plastic bags with trousers, jumpers, kagools and trainers. One after the other they handed over handfuls of cash. Loz was astonished at the amount of money they were seemingly pleased to hand over. They grabbed their bags, exited the shop and raced towards the tube station.

'So what's with all the casual gear then?' asked Loz.

'We're not going to be Mod's anymore, it's as simple as that. We have been Mod's since nineteen eighty and now something new is coming in. It don't mean we are going to start listening to Yazoo, Depeche Mode and all that old shit, it's just the clothes that's changing.'

'Okay, I understand. I like the look to but don't have that kind of money you just handed over the counter. The casual gear is so expensive.'

'Beg, borrow, steal my friend. Don't worry mate you'll find a way. Just pick up a few bits at a time. We only bought so much today because we have been saving up for this trip. I even flogged my T.V Lambretta to raise some extra funds and bought myself a few bits from out of 'Hucks' last week. The other thing is that now that we coming to footy regular we would stand out like sore thumbs on the terraces. Even the Chelsea Skinheads are swopping their boots and braces for track suits and trainers. You'll see what I mean when we get to the Bridge.'

As they descended the steps leading down into the tube station Loz schemed a way to raise some money so he too could buy some new clothes. He figured a few days work would put enough cash in his pocket to buy at least a pair of trousers and trainers. His polo shirts would have to get him by a bit longer. His problem would be finding work he told himself. The tube was waiting for them so they jumped aboard and retraced their journey back to Earls Court. The platform was packed with boys singing *From Stamford Bridge to Wembley, We'll keep the blue flag flying high.* Den and his mates instantly joined in with them and Loz pretended to mouth the words.

The tube snaked its way into Fulham Broadway and a hundred Chelsea fans jumped off the train in full voice. The singing continued as the blue army marched up the steps and spilled out onto the Fulham Road. The first thing Loz witnessed was two men fighting. Next there was some cheering, pushing and shuffling as a mounted Police officer charged into the crowd. Den grabbed hold of Loz's arm and pulled him out of harm's way. They set off down the Fulham Road. The air was thick with the smell of burgers and hot dogs and horse shit. The atmosphere was electric. They passed pubs with names like the White Hart and the Rising Sun which were packed with Chelsea fans singing Chelsea songs and shouting abuse at the away fans.

Loz marvelled at the sight of the massive Shed End white brick wall. He could hear singing coming from inside the ground. However, instead of heading directly towards gate thirteen Den turned right and walked down a street lined with cottages painted in yellows, pale blues and pinks. They didn't look like they belonged in the shadow of the mighty Shed wall. Den advised that Loz stick close because he spotted a group of twenty Luton boys.

'There are some of the M.I.G's.' whispered Den.

'M.I.G.'s.'Loz questioned.

'Men In Gear remember, Luton's firm.'

The M.I.G.'s stood with their arms folded dressed in tracksuits and Burberry trench coats. Most of them sported moustaches and mullets. They sneered at the Mod's as they walked passed but they didn't get a reaction. Instead Den ushered Loz and his gang towards a pub called The Imperial. The pub was perched on the corner of a dead end street and an army of Police Officers guarded the Kings Road.

As soon as they entered The Imperial Den shoved a handful of pound notes into Loz's palm and told him to get five pints of lager in. He assured him that he would have no problem getting served. Den and the others then darted off into the toilets.

Loz shrugged his shoulders and pushed his way towards the bar. He lent on the bar dangling the pound notes between his thumb and forefinger. A tall Skinhead with a tattoo of a tear falling from his eye stood to his right. A fattish boy in a yellow Pringle jumper stood to his left. Nobody paid him any attention.

Loz got served without any difficulty or questioning and was just handing over the money when the pub broke into song *'Zigger Zagger, Zigger Zagger, Oi Oi Oi'*, washed

over him. He felt like he was getting a Chelsea baptism and soaked it up.

A moment later Den and the others strolled out of the toilets completely transformed into casuals. They walked up to Loz and grabbed a pint of beer each. Loz looked each of them up and down realizing they had discarded their Moddy clothes and abandoned them in the toilets and replaced them with their new togs from Simons. He was amazed. They each looked fantastic in their new gear. Suddenly Loz realized that he was the only one who didn't blend in with the rest of the pub. It reinforced his determination to find a job, earn some money and buy some new clothes.

'You all look brilliant' said Loz.

'Cheers' replied Den taking a sip from his pint.

'What you going to do with your old clothes?'

'Leave them in the toilets.' Malc butted in.

'Yeah, we are hardly going to carry a bag full of clothes around the terraces are we?' said Mark casually before checking his watch for the third time in the last five minutes.

'But you had Monkey jackets, Sherman's....'

Den interjected with 'It don't matter Loz, don't worry.'

They gulped the rest of the beers down and ordered a second which they swiftly downed before staggering out of the pub. They walked a different route side by side a hoard of Chelsea fans. There was another scuffle between a few casuals and some M.I.G's where they joined the Fulham Road. A few coppers observed the brawl for a few seconds before deciding to step in. And even then they only separated the fighters and ordered them to walk away.

Den led the way to gate thirteen and Loz spotted the fences and he imagined the bootlaces hanging from them. They paid their few pounds ticket fees and pushed their way through the turnstiles. Loz could feel his heart pounding as he was swept along with the other fans making their way to the terraces. The fans sung Chelsea songs and it echoed and bounced off the walls. Den stuck close to Loz and directed him towards a cramped space on the terrace.

Loz was awestruck by the appearance of the crowds, the pitch, the players on it and the sight of the infamous corrugated iron roof over the Shed. The singing was loud and offensive and faces looked mean and willing. Den spent the next few minutes educating Loz on some of the faces and firms in the crowd. They are from Tunbridge

Wells he would inform or that's Wally and Willy. He also pointed to a tough looking bunch of about twelve older Skinheads and said they were relics from the nineteen seventies. Loz thought they were hardest bunch of people he had ever seen and felt a pity for the poor people whose heads had been cracked by them over the years.

Loz could hardly keep his eye on the game as the crowd swayed from side to side and backwards and forwards. He did however catch glimpses of his heroes Kerry Dixon, Pat Nevin and David Speedie. He was also impressed by Colin Lee's performance on the field of play. The Shed end sang *'Zigger Zagger Zigger Zagger Oi Oi Oi'* over and over again in amongst other Chelsea favourites. Loz tried his best to remember the words for future visits.

For the next hour he scrutinised the boys on the terraces as much he did the game. He trod in beer and piss and found himself on the end of a few fag burns but he loved every second of it. Chelsea scored and the Chelsea faithful roared with delight. This was followed by vigorous taunting of the away fans that numbered only a couple of thousand. They retaliated with threatening gesticulation and wanker signs. The Police chomped hot dogs and watched the match.

Ten minutes before the final whistle Loz noticed the older Skinheads and several casuals exiting the Shed. Den saw his observation and informed him that they were leaving so they could go and ambush the away fans as they left the ground. Loz asked if they could go with them but Den shook his head and told him not on this occasion but may be the next time they came up. He then asked Loz if he wanted to return for another game. Loz just grinned which said it all.

The train journey home seemed to take for ever. The train was packed full with people clutching shopping bags and looking tired. So many seats had been occupied that Loz's group had needed to sit separately. When the train reached Bromley the woman sitting next to Den got up and left so Loz jumped in her place so quick the seat was still warm.

'So good day or what?' Den asked.

'Fucking hell yeah, the best day yet.'

'And what did you think of the game?'

'Fantastic. I absolutely loved watching Dixon and Speedie. It was really strange being that close to them. Have you ever met any of them or anyone else famous for that matter?'

'I've not met any of the current squad but I have passed lots of old players. I've seen Ron 'Chopper' Harris, Peter Osgood and I saw Roy Bentley once. My favourite moment though was when I met Weller.'

'Fucking hell, really, where?' cried Loz.

'I was with Mark one day down the Kings Road. We were queuing up at this shoe store to get these new loafers that just come out. Anyway Mark nudges me and nods his head telling me to check out the bloke standing with his back to us. I hadn't noticed the bloke up until then. So, Mark mouths the words WELLER to me and I think fucking hell it is. The next moment he turns around and it is, its Paul Weller standing with Paolo Hewitt. They both clocked us, look us up and down then wink as if to say nice ones lads. It was fucking amazing and I'll never forget it.'

'That's an incredible story. I hope I meet Weller one day, or Paolo Hewitt for that matter I fucking love 'Beat Concerto''

'So have you met anyone famous before?'

Loz thought for a moment and was about to shake his head when he remembered that he had.

'Huh ha! I was walking into town one afternoon and just as I was passing the Hare and Hounds this swish looking Rolls Royce pulls up beside me and the window winds down. Next there's this gruff cockney accent asking me for directions for the Hazlitt theatre. I say go this way, then go that and he thanks me, winds up his window and drives off. It's only a few minutes later that it dawns on me that it was Mike Read from Runaround.'

Den smiled but looked unimpressed.

'So are you going to get some casual gear then?' asked Den.

'Yeah I want to I just need to get some dosh together. I need to find a job. I saw some really nice items of clobber today either in Simons or down the tube station or on the terraces.'

'Look I'll phone you in the week coz my uncle Arthur was looking for someone to help him on his window cleaning round. His getting a bit old now and needs somebody to carry the buckets and steady the ladder. I'll give him a bell and see what he says alright.'

'Yeah thanks Den. So what do think about all this casual stuff? Is it better than Mod?'

'No Loz it's not any better and it's not any worse. It's different but in some way it's Mods moving on. Mark my words within the year there won't be any Mods around. A year from now every teenage boy with a sense of style will be into the casual thing. It will not just stay on the terraces it will go mainstream. The trends will always start off on the terraces but over time they will filter through to every kid on every street corner. That's what happens to fashion at a working class level.'

'Right, I got yer. So yeah I'm going to save up some money and buy some clobber. I've seen some nice bits in 'Hucks' any way.'

'Yeah, they do have some nice bits but before long every kid around town will be dressed in the same get up. Being a casual means you have at least got to try and stay one step ahead of your mates. There's a shop in Chatham called 'El Tiba' why don't you try there. They stock all sorts of designer sports wear. They have some weird patchwork leather and suede smocks too called Robin Hoods but they're not my cuppa tea.'

'Okay, cheers. That would save the train fare to London too. I need to buy some trainers first. I keep seeing two kinds that seem to be the most popular. I mean every other casual had them on today. Do you know what they are called and who makes them?' Loz asked hopefully.

'The ones with either the blue or red tick are called 'Wimbledon's' or tennis and the others which come in blue, red or gold are Diadora Elites. But if you keep your eyes out you can pick up others. I'm still a big fan of Samba.'

'I love the Samba's too. I'll always believe them to be the classiest trainer ever made. I love the shape, the colour and the soft leather. Brilliant'.

Loz and Den continued to chat about casuals, Mod's, Chelsea and trainers for the remainder of the journey until the train pulled into their station. By this time the train was almost empty having unloaded most of its passengers at Bromley, Swanley and Sevenoaks. Malc noted that it was still only nine o clock so suggested they went for a drink in the Fishers Arms. Nobody put up a fight, especially Loz who didn't want the day to ever end. They left the train station behind and headed in the direction of the pub. They passed the rowdy Dragoon full of squaddies and then the more timid Flower Pot that looked like it only had half a dozen punters in it. Loz had never been inside the Fishers Arms. It was a traditional pub that left him feeling like he was sitting in someone's front room. The old Mod's come new casuals and Loz sat squeezed around a table avoiding the darts that were being tossed a few inches from where they sat. They drank more beer and ate prawn cocktail crisps. Loz felt accepted and over the moon. He went for a piss and on the way back bumped into Den who told him he wanted to show him something.

Loz followed Den into the pub courtyard. It was dark apart from a single spot light that Den twisted so that it shone its beam onto the white brick wall. Den nodded towards the wall and Loz strained his eyes to see what Den wanted him to look at. He could just about make out the faint letters of someone's name. 'That say's Mark, and that one Malc, Gus, hold on that's you.'

Loz then read out the names of several others and asked why they were written on the wall in row with two foot spaces between them. Den then explained that they were the individual parking slots for each of their scooters and had been painted on the wall a few years earlier when Malc use to live in the pub. Loz thought this was fantastic and thanked Den for showing him a bit of his town's Mod history.

A CASUAL AFFAIR

'It's been four weeks since the school holidays started Loz and you haven't done much about finding a job have you.' Loz's mum genuinely appeared to be cross with him.

He sipped his tea biding some thinking time then told her that he was still waiting to hear about the Y.T.S. job. She looked at him suspiciously then returned to cutting potatoes that she would be making one her delicious shepherd's pies with.

The kitchen radio was playing a song at low volume. Loz recognised it as Ultravox's hit single 'Vienna'. The song jogged his memory back to the days when a friend of the family whose name was Chris used to cycle down most days during one of the previous year's summer holidays. Whenever he showed up he had a collection of his seven inch singles hidden in his bag. Chris spent most of his pocket on buying records. His intention was to collect enough so that he could become a Dee jay.

The Ultravox song was one that Loz remembered Chris use to bring and play. Another song that always reminded Loz of those days with Chris was 'Embarrassment' by Madness and 'Do nothing' by the Specials, which had become Loz's all-time favourite Specials song.

The Ultravox song was still playing when Loz asked his mum a question.

'Do you ever feel jealous?' he asked.

His mum looked at him, thought for a few seconds then replied.

'Yes sometimes. I'm sure everybody does. Why?'

'No particular reason.'

Just then 'Rhinestone cowboy' began to play on the radio. Loz had not heard the song for years. The song was Loz's earliest memory of a piece of music. He held an image in his mind of being a toddler and walking along a street with his mum in the area where he lived up until the age of five. Loz smiled at his mum then left the kitchen.

It was another hot summer's day. It was as if the sun got hotter as each day of the school holidays passed. Loz was climbing up the hilly part of Boxley road when he heard the pop pop sound of a scooter's engine creep up behind him. As he turned to see who it was a blue PK 50 pulled up alongside him. Loz only recognised the rider when he removed his helmet.

'Fuck me alright mate, where did you get that from?'

It was one of Loz's oldest friends Jed or Jedi as he was fondly known. Jed and Loz were the same age and had gone to the same primary and secondary schools. For years Jed and his family had lived directly opposite Loz's house. Only Jed was never allowed to cross the street so he could only watch everyone play from the vantage point of the steps outside his house. Jed had a kind face with rosy cheeks and he had an enormous grin. He was wearing an army flight jacket, combats and Adidas boxing boots with red, white and blue stripes. He turned off the engine and placed his helmet on the Vespa seat.

'I got it for my sixteenth. Nice colour isn't it?

'Happy birthday and happy days then' said Loz 'I haven't seen you since the last day of school so what have you been up to?'

'More like what have you been up to 'Gobble Gobble Gobble'' Jed laughed.

'Bollocks.'

'Ha ha. I've been working with my dad in his kitchen fitting firm. It's a hard graft but we have work coming out of every hole so that's good. It keeps the old man happy anyway and means I get lots of work and loads of work means loads of money.'

'I don't suppose there's any job's going in your dad's firm is there?'

'No Loz sorry, there's no room, it's just me, my dad and Michael and Nathan'.

Loz expected Jed to say that and shrugged his shoulders.

'What's happened to your hair anyway?' Jed asked scrutinising Loz's new style.

'Just trying something different. Fuck me I've had a French line for years so I'm combing in the centre parting to get that Weller look on the 'Town Called Malice' video.'

'Right. It suits you.'

'Cheers. There's another Trinity disco soon. Are you coming to that one?'

'I might do. I could ride down on my scooter couldn't I? But I'll have to see nearer the time because sometimes we don't finish work until gone seven'.

'Seven, on a Friday, fuck that,' screamed Loz.

'You gotta do it if you want the reddies mate. Besides I'm thinking of saving for a mortgage and they don't come cheap.'

'A fucking mortgage! are you having a laugh you're only sixteen for fucks sake'.

'You take the piss now but when you're struggling to pay your mortgage off when you're sixty five I would have paid mine off years before and I'll be smiling.'

'Yeah I suppose you have got a point there.' Loz resigned.

'Any way I've got to shoot off.'

'Shoot off, on that, now you're having a laugh. Look, try to make the Trinity yeah. See you later.'

Loz waved Jed off and Jed left him with a nostril full of two stroke. Loz set off again in the direction of Gary's house which was near Peneden Heath. The Heath itself was a large area of grassy playing areas, a low rise building that was the toilets, the Bull pub and Arthur's café which only ever sold about a dozen different items. Nobody was spoilt for choice in Arthur's café. Behind the café was a well maintained gardens area with bowling greens, tennis courts and crazy golf or putty as it was called. Flanking the Heath was a woodland area where Loz had spent many hours as a child playing soldiers and constructing camps.

Peneden Heath was also famous for having a history of capital punishment. Near the clock there was a concrete slab about two metres square. All the local kids were taught that the concrete slab was the place where criminals from the prison in town were bought to and hung. Loz had been told the last woman in England had been hung on that spot. Loz never knew if it was true. The stories of public hangings gave rise to many ghost stories however and the Heath was certainly a scary place to be on a foggy winter's night.

Loz strolled over the concrete slab arrogantly whilst watching a game of headers and volleys that a bunch of kids were getting stuck into. He skirted the pub and crossed the road that led to Boxley village. Five minutes later Loz was knocking on the door of Gary's house. A tall thick set grey haired man who looked like he was built to play rugby opened the door and looked at the skinny specimen in front of him.

'Hello' he said in a deep Yorkshire accent.

'Hello, hmm, is Gary home please?'

The towering Yorkshire warrior looked sternly at him and then the muscles in his face relaxed.

'Yes come in lad, he is down in his pit. Follow me.'

Loz followed him down a set of stairs until he reached a door which he pushed open.

'Here's your new friend Gary.' He announced and pushed Loz into the bedroom.

Gary stood up wearing a pair of olive green jumbo cords and a black tracksuit top with red piping around the cuffs and collar. His bedroom was small with inbuilt wardrobes with mirrors. One of the wardrobe doors was open and Loz glanced inside noticing a row of tracksuits and tee-shirts. It was an impressive collection of designer sportswear that Loz hoped to match in time.

'You have an impressive wardrobe mate' said Loz.

'Cheers. I've been collecting for a couple of years.'

'How did you get into the whole casual thing?' Loz asked.

'All my mates got into it mostly because of their older brothers really.'

'Because of football,' Loz interrupted.

'Yeah. My mate's brothers either went to Elland Road or Valley Parade. Some of them were members of the L.S.C. Leeds Service Crew. But I had a bunch of friends who lived in a small village called Cleckheaton or Clecky as we called it. They were Andy and Gaz the bone. We started off with the samba, cords and snorkel coat look. Ideal for the freezing Yorkshire winters on the terraces. Then we started to introduce the sportswear.'

'Right okay. But I have to ask what is this shit that you're playing on the record player?'

'Breakdance-Electric Boogaloo. From the film.'

'It's bollocks.'

Gary laughed then added 'I don't suppose you have been to see the film have you?'

'No chance, it's not my cup of tea mate. I can't get my head around all that electronic stuff, you know drum machines and all that. Give me Steve White any day.'

'But it's fresh and new and it's the way music is going. Before long the charts will be dominated with drum machines and keyboards.'

Gary stood in front of one of the mirrors brushing his big floppy wedge. He jolted his head and the flick of his wedge swooshed about.

'I still don't like it. I do like you're cords though. Where did you get them?'

Gary thought for a moment then answered 'Manchester's underground market a couple of months before I moved down here. I bought a burgundy pair too'.

'I went to Simon's in Shepherds the other day. They have all the latest gear'.

'No they have all the last gear. The casuals up north have been wearing that stuff for months before it ends up down south.'

'I'm not sure about that.' Loz protested.

'It's true. The whole terrace culture started up north. Only up north nobody called themselves casuals. They used named like Dressers or Perry boys. Casuals is a southern thing'. He spoke with a sense of authority on the matter and Loz shrunk.

'Well anyway there were some nice jeans in Simons.'

'Did you buy anything?' asked Gary looking up as he tied the laces on his trainers.

'No but I'm going to save up some money and buy a few bit's. In fact I thought today we could go to Chatham and check out this new shop called El Tibas that I'm told stocks all the latest gear. Fancy it?'

Gary agreed and they set off to Reece's house. They crossed the Heath and instead of climbing up Boxley Road they took a shortcut through what the locals termed 'shit alley' on account of the amount of white dog shit they would have to avoid treading in. The alley was narrow and long and they spent the entire journey batting away small flies. Loz and Gary continued to argue about music and casuals. At one point there was break in the alley and small stretch of wall with a doorway carved out of it. Whenever Loz passed this he would always remember his first 'proper' girlfriend. She lived nearby. After school Loz would walk his girlfriend home, but only as far as that part of the alley. They would then snog and Loz would give her the middle finger. It was a bit risky because the alley was well used with other school children and parents but in the three months they went out together they never got caught. Sometimes Jed use to walk with them and had to wait around the corner until Loz had finished with his handy work. The memory always caused Loz to chuckle.

They left the alley and crossed the road. Next they passed an old gothic looking church and stopped at a house a few yards from the church. Gary pushed the gate open and they walked along the path to the front door. Gary rang the doorbell. Inside a dog barked and a few seconds later the door swung open. A tall boy with pale skin and blonde spikey hair barred their way. There was a moment's hesitation between them and then the boy beckoned them inside. He shouted 'Door' up the stairs and left Loz and Gary hovering in the hallway.

'That's Reece's brother Steve' informed Gary.

'He dont seem that friendly.'

'No he is okay. He was in a video you know.'

'What kind of video?' asked Loz.

'It was the music video of Bauhaus's version of Ziggy Stardust. Steve is standing in a corridor as the band pass through it.'

'Wow' was all Loz could muster as a response.

Just then a woman poked her head around the corner to see who had entered her house. 'It's alright Bob' she shouted back into the room where she had come from 'It's only Reece's new friends. Hello boys I'm Reece's mum. Go up if you like. Top of the stairs then turn left, turn right and then right again' she said with a kind smile.

Gary went first. At the top of the stairs they followed the directions to Reece's room and knocked on the closed door. Reece opened it and music burst out. He invited them inside.

'Fuck me this is a bit strong aint it,' cried Loz.

Every wall in the bedroom had been painted a matt black. Even the curtains were black. The legs of Reece's bed had been removed and the only furniture in the room was a tatty pull out sofa bed, a wardrobe and a record player. Dozens of albums were scattered over the floor along with items of clothing. There were several empty wine bottles that had been turned into candle holders and had different colour waxes stuck to the side of them.

Reece invited them to sit on the tatty sofa so they flopped down onto it. Loz sifted through some of the albums on the floor. They were albums from bands like The Smiths, Joy Division and Japan.

'That's my favourite band.' Reece informed nodding to the Japan album.

'Okay' said Loz before his attention was drawn to an album sleeve with a picture of a big yellow banana on it.

'What's this?'

'A band from the sixties New York scene called the Velvet Underground. The albums actually called Andy Warhol after the artist.'

Loz shook his head letting Reece know he had not heard of either.

'Loz wants to go to Chatham is that ok?' asked Gary.

'Yes. Why?' said Reece.

'There's a shop there that sales trainers and tracksuits' added Loz.

Reece then continued to get dressed. He slipped a yellow polo shirt over his skinny chest and adjusted the velcro strap on his trainers.

The three boys walked into town pass the Trinity church and down into the bus station that was connected to the Stoneborough shopping centre. Although the bus station was noisy, echoed and was filthy Loz was always felt an air of excitement in the bus station.

Their double decker green bus was already waiting so they jumped on it, paid their fare's and climbed the steps to the top deck where they raced to the front seats and peered down at the shoppers trying to avoid getting run over by the buses as they dragged their shopping bags along.

The bus journey took thirty minutes. It snaked through the town centre, went up Boxley Road and along Sandling Road before merging with the Bluebell hill. It spent ten minutes struggling up the hill that Loz had travelled up the day he was the passenger on the back of Den's scooter. Once in Chatham the bus stopped a few more times to pick up passengers before finally arriving at the Pentagon shopping centre.

Loz jumped off the bus and followed the directions to El Tiba's that Den had given him. They passed a record store that Loz had once bought a Japanese import of the Jam's *'Eton rifles'* from, then a bakers where the cream donuts looked tasty and other cheap looking clothes shops until they left the Pentagon centre took a sharp left and there in front of them was El Tiba's.

The three boys slowly approached the shop scanning the items in the shop window. There were tracksuits of every designer sportswear hanging up in every colour under the sun. With eyes and mouths wide open they entered the Aladdin's cave of clobber.

A friendly Turkish looking man welcomed them into his shop. He had a chunky gold chain hanging from around his neck and he wore one the leather and suede smocks that Loz now knew were called Robin Hoods. Loz actually thought they looked quite good now that he had seen one in the flesh.

'Are you looking for anything in particular?' asked the Turk.

'Whatever fifty pounds can get me really' replied Loz.

'Ah my friend, you will find something for fifty pounds. Look at the tracksuits on that rail.'

Gary and Reece were already checking through the items on the rail in question. Loz joined in with the hunt. There were some nice velour track suit tops but they were too expensive at seventy pounds. Then Gary snatched a black and yellow Tachinni tracksuit top from the rail and held it up. Loz instantly fell in love with it and the price was right. Gary told Loz to try it on. Loz took the tracksuit top from him and carefully put it on savouring every moment of the experience. The cotton material was smooth and the item smelt new and fresh. Reece and Gary nodded approvingly and Loz looked at himself in the mirror. He tucked his hands into the side pockets and adopted a posture where he imagined himself standing on the terraces of the Shed End alongside the Chelsea casuals.

'It suits you my friend' said the Turk crashing into Loz's daydream.

'It's the one mate' added Gary and Reece agreed.

'I'll have it,' announced Loz and stepped over to the Turk and handed him forty eight pounds. The Turk handed him back his change and Loz looked at it thinking at least he had enough for a cream donut. Meanwhile Gary and Reece had been exploring the Robin Hoods. Gary was serious about getting one of the rustic looking smocks and said that they would go well with a pair of white trainers and a pair of his Sharpe cords.

Loz only half paid attention, he was too excited about having purchased his first item of casual clobber. He knew he was well and truly on his way now to a brave new world. The Turk waved them goodbye as they left the shop and strolled back into the Pentagon shopping centre. Loz clutched his El Tiba bag proudly. They walked around the Pentagon eyeing up the local Chatham girls in their short skirts and they went to the bakers where Loz bought a loaf of bread instead of a cream donut and spent the next twenty minutes eating it up. Reece said he wanted to check out the record shop they had passed on their arrival so Loz led the way back to it.

The record shop was narrow but long. *'Sixty eight guns'* by The Alarm was blasting out through the speakers as they entered. The three boys dispersed throughout the shop. Loz searched through posters of bands and films whilst Gary flicked through the Hip Hop section. Reece concentrated on the J section and found a signed copy of a Japan album which he bought. Gary also left the shop with a twelve inch version of Chaka Khan's *'Ain't nobody'*.

In the bus station they saw a double decker bus about to set off that had Boxley road written on the destination notice above the bus drivers head.

'Come on quick' Loz screamed and jumped on the bus.

They raced to the upper deck and claimed the seats at the front as their own. Loz removed his new Tracksuit top from the El Tiba bag and dangled it in the air whilst admiring it. Reece lovingly traced the signatures of the Japan band members with his index finger and Gary ogled the girls outside through the window. The bus roared down a ramp and into the main street. Loz opened one of the windows to let some fresh air into the stifling hot bus. Gary and Reece read out the various bits of graffiti that had been either scratched on written onto the seats and bus fittings. They laughed out loud as they read out 'Brian is bent', 'Tracey done a rugby team', 'West Ham' and 'NF'.

The bus seemed to stop every few hundred yards to pick up more passengers and took a different route to the one they had entered Chatham by. Loz thought that was odd but didn't say anything to the others. Then from out of nowhere Gary cried.

'Fruit picking!'

'Fruit picking!' said Loz curiously.

'You were saying earlier that you needed to get some work so that you can get some money to buy some more casual gear right.'

'Yes, I'm listening.'

'Well fruit picking. I'll do it too coz I saw a nice velour tracksuit back there that I fancy,' said Gary

'Me too coz I liked the look of a bright red one,' Reece added.

'I liked everything in the shop.' laughed Loz.

'So fruit picking. It's the time of year for strawberries, apples and pears. I reckon we should check the South Messenger and see what farms are advertising fruit picking jobs.

I've been told before that if you work hard you can earn up to fifty pounds a day. So imagine the money we could earn in two or three weeks of fruit picking.'

'Fucking hell yeah. We could certainly get enough dosh together to buy a couple of tracksuits, Farah's and trainers. That's a brilliant idea. Let's buy a copy of the S.M, when we get back into town.'

They were still discussing the benefits of becoming fruit farm labourers when the bus stopped in a deserted country road with rows of tall trees on both sides. The bus fell silent as the engine was turned off. The three boys sensed that something was not right. They had no idea where they were and they were the only ones left on the top deck. They sat for a few more minutes thinking the bus must be ahead of schedule or waiting to swop bus drivers. The bus was eerily quiet.

'This is a bit strange' said Loz.

'Yeah, the fucking bus must have broken down or something lets go ask the bus driver.' replied Reece looking concerned.

They grabbed their bags and made their way down the narrow steps to the lower deck which was also empty of passengers. They approached the bus driver who was curled up in his seat almost ready to doze off. He jumped when he saw the three boys glaring at him.

'Is there a problem?' asked Reece.

'Has the bus broken down or something?' Loz added.

'No lads.' replied the bus driver with a surprised expression on his face before continuing with. 'I didn't know anybody was left on the bus. This is far as the bus goes lad's'.

Loz, Gary and Reece looked confusingly at each other and then at the bus driver who stared back at them.

'But you're not in Boxley Road yet' quizzed Reece.

'Yes I am' returned the bus driver.

'No you're not' argued Reece.

'YES I am. This Boxley Road. The Boxley Road in Walderslade'.

Loz, Gary and Reece looked at one another again realizing their mistake. They had jumped on the wrong bus.

'Bollocks. Bollocks.' hissed Reece.

'It has got to be twelve miles or more back to town' groaned Loz.

'It is three miles to the top of Bluebell hill and then another eight to the bottom.' informed the bus driver with a grin.

'Come on then' sighed Gary, 'We have no choice we have got no more money so we will have to walk it.'

They stepped off the bus and headed in the direction of Bluebell hill. They cursed their foolishness and the road sign at the end of a two mile walk that announced 'Boxley Road'.

'Well at least it's downhill once we reach Bluebell hill'. Loz joked.

Reece was not impressed. It was three in the afternoon. It was hot, sunny and dry. The first few miles were tolerable but now they were feeling hungry and thirsty. Loz was less hungry having consumed the loaf of bread earlier but he was gasping for a drink having not drunken anything since his cup of tea at breakfast.

It was evident after two hours of walking that Reece was pissed off. He cursed everything and walked twenty paces behind Loz and Gary. They had to walk down a narrow bumpy path at the foot of the bright white chalky rock surface of the hills that flanked Bluebell hill. The brilliant white chalk reflected more of the sun's heat at them. Reece vowed never to return to Chatham. Loz felt partially responsible and tried to apologise but Reece couldn't give a shit.

The view from Bluebell hill was magnificent. From their vantage point they could see for miles. There was mile after mile of lush green fields, farm houses, villages and in the far distance the town they were heading for. Loz turned to Gary.

'Have you ever heard about the ghost of Bluebell hill?' he said.

'Ghost! No what's the story then?'

'The story is that a young woman died in a car accident coming down Bluebell hill, I think in the nineteen forties or fifties but I'm not certain. Anyway, there have been loads of accounts of lone male drivers picking up a young female hitchhiker down this stretch of the Bluebell hill. It always happens at night time and usually when it's cold and raining. That's why the drivers pick her up. You know out of pity. Then the woman jumps in the passenger seat and the driver set's off. But by the time they reach the bottom of the hill the young woman has vanished.'

'That's bollocks' frowned Gary.

'Might be but I'm telling you there have been loads of stories about it' Loz defended.

'Anyway, where are all the fucking Bluebells?' they both laughed.

The weary travellers walked on in silence. Reece was now thirty paces behind them.

'My aunty Pat in Bradford lives in the house where those photographs of the fairies with that small girl were taken in the garden' said Gary.

Loz thought for a moment then said 'What the ones that Conan Doyle took. That's right isn't it? The same bloke that wrote Sherlock Holmes.'

'I dunno know about that. Perhaps we should go and visit her. You would like that. Have you ever been to Yorkshire?'

'No, never. Furthest I've been is to Watford. So do you mean go up for a weekend or something with your family?'

'No. We could get the train from Victoria station. It's not that expensive. I could take you to meet my mates in Clecky and see some true dressers. And maybe even introduce you to one of the top boys whose name is Chimmy. We can go to Harry

Ramsdens to get the best fish and chips in the world and I'll treat you Yorkshire custard slices, the tastiest cakes in the world. How does that sound?'

'Sound's brilliant. Let's arrange it. But I want to see the fairies in your aunt's garden too.'

Gary laughed. An hour later they eventually reached Peneden Heath. Loz and Gary sat on a brick wall by a row of shops and waited for Reece to catch up. All three were need of a bath, a drink and some food. The three friends looked at the sign post nailed to the wall. It read Boxley Road and then burst into fits of laughter. They said their goodbyes and dispersed in three different directions to go home.

THANKFULLY NOT LIVING IN YORKSHIRE

The tall burly Yorkshire man casually opened the door. Loz and Gary's dad had met a few times now but he still enjoyed trying to playfully intimidate Gary's guests.

'Alright lad' he said 'Are you looking forward to going up to Yorkshire? Make sure our Gary takes you to Harry Rams, they do the best fish and chips in the world.'

And with that he admitted Loz into his castle and directed to him to go down to Gary's bedroom. Loz found Gary playing his Chaka Khan record that he had bought in Chatham. Loz actually liked the song but didn't let on to Gary.

'Alright Loz, I'm just sorting out a few bits of clobber for you to borrow.'

'Nice one mate.'

Loz searched through the pile of clothes that Gary had earmarked to loan him on their trip to Yokrshire. Loz held up a blue jumper to check if it would fit him. He decided it would be little baggy but it didn't matter he had eagerly accepted Gary's offer of clobber loan because he didn't want to meet Gary's mates dressed like a Mod.

'Right there you go put them in that bag will you' said Gary.

He pointed to a leather holdall. Loz picked up the tee shirts and jumper and carefully laid them in the holdall.

'We have got two hours before we need to catch the train to London. My dad said he will drop us off down the station so we have time to nip round the estate and see Les and the others.'

'Okay' replied Loz and they set off for the estate.

It was only a ten minute walk to the estate via alleyways and shortcuts until they arrived at Les's house. Les was standing on his doorstep wearing his faded Fiorucci jeans with frayed bottoms, white trainers and a pink Lacoste tee shirt. He was clutching a woollen jumper. Les was standing next to a man who appeared to be in his early twenties. The man looked like the rough and ready sort with a perm come mullet and was dressed in yellow trainers, faded jeans with slits in the bottom and a pale green Fila tee shirt.

'Alright boys' said Les, 'This is my uncle.'

The uncle greeted them with a wink. Loz and Gary were pleased to finally meet Les's uncle. They had heard a great deal about him. He lived in West Ham and was a member of West Ham's firm the I.C.F. Les's uncle had also been responsible for Les's extensive casual wardrobe because whenever he visited he would bring with him bags of clobber that he had 'acquired'.

'Look at what my uncles brought me' said Les.

Les held up a green and brown rustic coloured woollen crew neck jumper. It looked coarse and heavy but stylish and perfect for the terraces in the autumn and winter months. Loz leaned forward to read the label inside. The label read Sabro. Loz reminded himself that he needed to remember the name.

'What are you up to anyway?' asked Les.

'Just killing some time before we catch the train to London' replied Gary.

Les's uncle heard the Yorkshire accent.

'Where are you from then?' he asked.

'Yorkshire!'

'Who do you support then?' the uncle quizzed.

'Leeds United' boasted Gary.

'Leeds, Leeds, Leeds, Leeds'. chanted the uncle.

Gary took a step back and Les and Loz giggled.

'Scary place Elland road. I've had a few run in's with the L.S.C.'

'What's been your scariest away day?' chipped in Les.

'There's a few Les. The Den of course because there is fierce rivalry between us and Millwall. Then there's Griffin Park, Maine Road and Chelsea. Spurs are a bit tasty as well.'

The three boys lapped up every word and looked on in awe. Les's uncle then said he needed to be setting off so he said his goodbyes and jumped into his black Capri which had furry dice hanging from the inside mirror and sped off. Loz, Gary and Les walked along the street through an alley way and entered a tunnel that smelt of piss and sheep shit. A few empty glue sniffers bags lay discarded on the floor and the concrete walls of the tunnel were covered in graffiti. A dozen different versions of the words The Jam dominated the graffiti. The tunnel led to an open grassy field that slopped away. It had a tiny stream at the bottom of it. The place was known as the sheepwash

Loz had spent many misspent moments at the sheepwash. He had paddled in the stream numerous times and had freed tadpoles into it a few times as well. The previous winter had been an especially cold and snowy one and this had made the Sheepwash the perfect location for sledging. Lots of local kids had shared the Sheepwash for their hours of sledging pleasure. That winter had been Loz's first sledging experience. He had enjoyed every second of it. The wrapping up warm, the dragging the sledge to the brow of the hill and then sledging off gathering great speeds and then taking off into the air and landing in the icy stream.

The only time to avoid the Sheepwash was when the local farmer allowed his bull's to roam around it. There were no bulls today. Or sheep for that matter and the three boys climbed over the sty and entered the field. On the far side of the field they could see some more of their friends.

They walked beside the stream until they reached the others. There were three girls Shirley who was tall and attractive and then Esther and Clare who were twins with long straight blonde hair. The twins were originally from London. They had a London charm. Loz liked the sisters, they were friendly and fun to be with. Behind the girls stood Steve who Loz had not seen since the Howard Wardell disco the night after the last day of school.

'How's it going?' asked Steve.

'Yeah alright! How comes your tanned then?' replied Loz.

'I've been doing some roofing with my brother Lee. It gets hot up on them roofs. Fuck doing roofing for a living.'

'Are you excited about your trip to Gary's neck of the woods?' butted in Shirley.

'Yeah I am. I've never been up north before. It's gonna be a laugh. What are you all doing anyway?'

'Steve is trying to catch frogs' answered Esther.

'Why?' asked Gary.

'So that he can pull their legs off' replied Clare.

Loz was not surprised. He expected this type of behaviour from Steve.

The group then spent the next hour killing time in the Sheepwash. Steve didn't find or catch any frogs. They were all of similar age and had the same issues and problems to discuss. Finding a job fuelled the most heated debate. It was evident that they all felt sad about leaving school too. Only the twins had a year left to enjoy.

The time arrived for Loz and Gary to leave so that they could catch their train without having to rush. They said their goodbyes and a see you soon at the next Trinity disco and departed. When they returned to Gary's house his dad was waiting at the door. Loz rushed to Gary's bedroom where he quickly replaced his clothes with some of Gary's and then they loaded the car with their bags and were dropped off at the train station. Gary's dad's final words were 'Harry Rams'.

The train took an hour to reach Victoria. The National Express coach to Bradford took much longer. Both boys slept most of the journey. Loz felt very excited. He had never done anything that required so much confidence and sensibility before. He thought his mum and dad would have put up more resistance to allowing him to go but they didn't. He assumed he had gained their trust that he could be sensible and responsible. Loz's dad had even given him some spending money.

Yorkshire looked a different world to Loz with its hilly expansive landscape. Gary's eyes lit up. Yorkshire was still his home inside. The coach dropped them off in Leeds and it had been arranged that Gary's uncle Phil would pick them up outside the bus station. The two boys collected their bags and headed for the meeting point.

'Now a word of advic.' began Gary 'If a lad asks you the time ignore him.'

'Why? I don't understand' said a confused Loz.

'It happens at footy all the time. It's a way of finding out where you're from. The person isn't really interested what the time is, they are trying to find out if you are from Leeds, Burnley, London and so on. It's a technique the firms have always used to sniff out the enemy.'

Loz thanked Gary for giving him the heads up. They walked down a tunnel that exited the bus station and as they did a lone youth with a skinhead but dressed to the nines in top casual gear passed them. As he passed he looked at Loz with an inquisitive eye. Loz was sure the Skinhead was going to ask him the time. He didn't and Loz released a sigh of relief.

Uncle Phil was waiting for them with the car engine running. He was a tall dark haired man and friendly. They jumped in the car and he drove them to his house in Bradford. The house was modern. The first thing Gary's aunty Pat mentioned was the fairies at the bottom of the garden. They had tea, got bathed and went to bed early. Loz and Gary were preparing themselves for a fun packed couple of days.

The two boys awoke early, were force fed a hearty breakfast and dropped off at a bus stop at the bottom of the hill. Ten minutes later the bus arrived and took them to Cleckheaton.

'First off Loz is the baker's shop.' said Gary.

Once they arrived in the village of Cleckheaton Gary made a bee line for the bakers. The bakers smelt great with its shelves stacked with Bloomers and Cobs. There was a smell that reminded Loz of his other Nan's house. She made flat round loaves of bread that were delicious and whenever his dad went to visit her he would always return with a few loaves of his mums bread. Gary ignored the aroma and loaves and pointed to two custard slices.

'Here, eat this, it's the best cake in the world' said Gary offering Loz the custard creation.

'Mmmm, that is fucking delicious mate.'

Loz had never tasted a cake so delicious and went back into the shop and bought two more. The two boys were just finishing them off when one of Gary's old friends Carree turned the corner. He looked stunned and surprised to see Gary sitting outside the bakers in his village with custard all around his mouth.

'Fuck me. What are you doing here?' said Carree.

'I'm up here for two day's with my mate from down south Loz. Loz meet Alfie Carr but we call him Carree.'

Loz and Carree exchanged greetings and Carree sat on the step next to them. Gary enquired about his other friends and an old girlfriend and Carree did his best to update Gary on all the latest news. He added that Gary's old girlfriend still pined for him and had not had a new boyfriend since he had moved down south. This seemed to please Gary.

'So where are going next?' asked Gary.

'I was on my way to see Gaz.'

'Brilliant, Gaz the bone, we will come with you.'

They set off and walked passed cottages and council houses until they arrived at Gaz the bones house. There were a few steps that led down into a long narrow garden path. They walked along it and opened the porch door. Loz noticed a pair of tatty

Samba trainers discarded on the floor. Carree knocked several times but there appeared to be nobody home. Carree suggested they try the pub down the road because Gaz the bone sometimes hid out in their when he was bored.

Carree led the way to the pub and they went inside. Gaz the bone was sitting at a table with a couple of other boys. He was as surprised to see Gary as much as Carree had been. A round of greetings and introductions commenced and few pints of beer were ordered. Gary and his friends chatted energetically about other mutual friends, Leeds United, Bradford town and girls. They also showed an interest in what the casuals were wearing down south. Gary helped Loz to explain.

'What's coming in for the autumn?' Gary asked Gaz the bone.

'Eighteen inch flares, Samba's, deer stalkers.'

'Deer stalkers, elementary dear Gaz the bone' remarked Loz feeling a little pissed.

Nobody appeared to get the joke and Gaz the bone continued.

'Crew neck wool jumpers and hooded corduroy jackets that you can get in the Manchester underground market.'

'And bobble ski hats will be in for the winter for sure,' added Carree.

'Oh and Cez Geer have a limited range called G2. They have some really nice jumpers.' added Gaz the bone.

Loz could really sense the differences between the dressers up north and the casuals down south. He thought it would be ideal to mix the two styles up. Gary appeared to have the same idea and they decided they would visit Manchester the following day. They were downing their third pint when a young man about twenty walked into the pub. He had a wedge and wore a denim coat, jeans and crew neck jumper. Gaz the bone got up and went to speak with the young man. Carree explained that the man's name was Chimmy and he was one of the Leeds Service crew's top boys.

Gaz the bone returned a few minutes later but Chimmy left the pub. Gaz the bone then filled the others in on the details relating to their away day to Derby on Saturday. Loz was fascinated by the conversation. At seven o clock Loz and Gary had to leave the pub and catch the return bus to Bradford. Before leaving Loz invited both Gaz the bone and Carree to Kent. They accepted the invitation.

The following morning Loz and Gary got up early again and were again dropped off at the bus stop. Only this time they went to Leeds. Gary wanted to take Loz to a shop that sold only trainers. They reached Leeds in good time and headed straight for the trainer shop. Whereas El Tiba's had been a treasure trove of togs the trainer shop was ten times more impressive. The Ceiling to the floor was full of shelves of trainers from every sports designer the list was endless. Gary was in his element because he truly loved trainers. Loz was equally impressed and found a pair of yellow trainers in the sale. They had blue stripes and blue soles and looked fantastic. Gary saw Loz fondling the trainers.

'How much?'

'Thirty,' replied Loz.

'You gonna get them. I would if I was you. Try them on.' And with that he called over one of the shop workers and asked her to go and get the other shoe. She returned a few moments later and Loz tried the trainers on. They felt great. They were light and wrapped themselves around Loz's foot perfectly. Loz bought his first pair of casual's trainer and wore them for the rest of the day. He felt like he was walking on air.

Gary wanted to buy some trainers to but said he would wait until they got to Manchester in case he saw some things there he wanted instead. They left the trainer shop and headed for the train station where they caught the train to Manchester. Loz was having the time of his life. He was experiencing new towns and cities, making new friends and had just notched himself up the ladder of style.

Manchester was busy and crowded. On exiting the train station the first thing to catch Loz's attention was a man collecting money for the miners. This was something that Loz had not seen before. It brought home to him the reality of the suffering miners. The image of that man collecting money stayed with Loz. Gary warned Loz to keep his wits about him in the underground market. He said it had a reputation for attracting unsavoury lads.

Loz had never experienced a market like it. The stalls were full of trendy and stylish clothes not the cheap tatty stuff he was use to in the markets nearer to home. Even Petticoat Lane had nothing on this place. Gary led the way weaving in and out of the aisles until he stumbled over the stall that sold the corduroy jackets that Gaz the bone had told him about. Gary knew he would have to buy one now even though it was still the peak of summer. He tried on a dark brown one and it looked great on him. He handed a Ddrk green one to Loz who tried it on. They both looked at each other and decided they needed to get them.

'Nobody back home will have these coats' said Gary.

'Oh yeah! We will definitely turn some of the heads of the older boys' replied Loz.

So they bought the coats and Gary bought a pair of flares as well. Just as they were about to leave Loz turned around and said he was going to buy some flares to. So he did and spent all his money. They left Manchester behind and returned to Leeds. Before they caught the bus back to Gary's aunts he treated Loz to a portion of Harry Rams fish and chips. Loz thought they were only alright.

PRETTY GREEN

'Bloody hell Loz, you look like a lobster' cried Robert.

Robert was swinging on one of the swings in the play area near the Howard Wardell. Loz approached him wearing his new yellow trainers. Robert appeared to pay no attention.

'Yeah well it's better than smelling like one. But you would know, you still giving that pikey bird a good licking?' Loz fired back.

'Ha ha, funny, but no I haven't. I only saw her a couple of times before I got scared off by her brothers. Mind you she was a handful if you get my drift'.

'I know of her brothers. If they are not fighting with the squaddies they are fighting amongst themselves. I remember the older brother got into a fight outside Mr Wimpo's one day. There were four Geordie squaddies and just him. They gave him a right pasting and at the end of it he got to his feet and yelled at them 'Is that the best you can do?'

'But seriously how comes you are so red?'

'Well if you're that interested to know I've been spending this week fruit picking.' Loz revealed.

'What are you doing that for then?'

'Because I need to get some cash to buy some things.'

'What kind of things?' pressed Robert.

'Fuck me what is this twenty questions or something. I just need some money to buy some new clobber.'

'Nice one, so you're going to heading back off to Carnaby Street then?'

'Not exactly,' replied Loz losing interest in the conversation.

'Okay.'

'Any way how was your holiday? Did you manage to screw any old boilers?' Loz teased.

'Well I did pull this German bird called Anka. She was pretty but a little plump. It must be all the sausage they eat. It was going alright and we having a snog and I was groping her tits. Then she lifted her arm up and I got an eyeful of her hairy arm pits. Hairy fucking arm pits like a woolly mammoths arse. Well it turned me right off. I couldn't help thinking what her downstairs would be like if her arm pits were anything to go on. I imagined it would like a fucking jungle down there and I would never find the hole. Mind you she knew every word to *Ninety nine red balloons*.'

The two of them fell about laughing. Loz then told Robert about his trip up north, his day out in Chatham and the long walk home and his fruit picking job.

'Has anything more happened about the bonehead's car?' enquired Robert.

Loz shook his head. He hadn't heard anything about it and that had troubled him. Loz knew that the fight down the Wander Inn could have been forgotten with time but the destruction of the Cortina meant the Skinheads would definately be on the war path. There was no way they would forget about that. Loz also knew that whoever they caught up with first would be introduced to a whole new world of pain. He just hoped it wouldn't be him.

'Look I've got to go mate so I'll see you down the Trinity alright' said Loz.

'Oh ok. Where are you off to now then?'

'My dad's is giving me a lift somewhere.'

'Okay, fair enough, I'll see you later then. Oh and by the way those trainers are a bit bright aint they?'

Loz walked off after sticking two fingers up at his friend.

As Loz turned the corner of his street he peered inside the Post Office. Mr Patel was selling an orange ice lolly and a chocolate bar to two children. He waved at Loz and Loz returned the wave. Loz had already spotted his dad washing his Viva outside the house. He had his Royal Mail shirt on with the sleeves rolled up.

'Alright boy. Are you ready?'

Loz noticed the faint traces of his dad's Hartlepool accent. Loz hardly ever noticed but his friends were often commenting on it.

'Yes dad. I'm ready to go when you are.'

Loz's dad tipped the dirty water down the drain then bundled the bucket and sponges into the boot of the car.

'How's the fruit picking going?' Loz's dad asked as they drove down the street.

'It's okay actually but it can be a hard graft when the midday sun is beating down. My back hurts a bit.'

'Anything on the horizon regards a proper job?'

'Only the Y.T.S position up at Dutton's.'

'Why don't you fill in an application form for the Royal Mail?' said Loz's dad fiddling with the car stereo.

'Maybe' replied Loz and the conversation dried up. Loz was grateful that his dad never piled on the pressure to do this or do that. His dad had always given him the space to find his own way and make his own mistakes.

Once they arrived in Chatham Loz's dad pulled into the large car park opposite the Pentagon shopping centre. He turned off the engine and removed his golden tobacco tin from his trouser pocket. Loz was about to jump out of the car but his dad asked him if he could hang on for five minutes because he had something to give him. Loz waited patiently and curiously. Loz's dad rolled the fag and lit it with a clipper lighter before handing Loz a Brown envelope.

'What is it?' asked Loz accepting the envelope.

'Have a look.' said his dad smiling.

Loz torn open the envelope 'Bloody hell!' he exclaimed.

'It's yours.'

'There's got to be three hundred quid in here' cried Loz.

'Your mum and me have been putting a few quid into a savings account for you and now it's matured so we opted to cash it in now. So it's your money and you can spend it on what you want.'

'Bloody hell' Said Loz again 'I don't know what to say, but thanks, really thanks. I'll get mum a box of chocolates and a Neil Diamond album or something.'

Loz stepped out of the car clutching the envelope of cash and beaming the biggest smile in Chatham. He tried to work out the maths on the money he already had from the fruit picking and the unexpected three hundred. He bounced all the way to El Tiba's. The Turkish shop owner recognised him and greeted him enthusiastically. Loz made a bee line for the section with the trainers and grabbed a pair of gold Diadora Elites. Next he searched through the Fila tracksuit tops and picked one out in blue and white that he thought would advertise that he was a Chelsea fan. Then he selected a pair of pale blue Farah trousers and asked the shop keeper if he had some in a twenty eight waist. The Turk scurried off into a room behind the counter and returned a few moments later dangling the trousers in the air and licking his lips. Loz was already waiting at the counter and counting out his money. He also added a blue and white Gabicci sweatshirt and a Patrick kagool to the pile.

The Turk accepted the money and counted it before slapping it into his money belt and handing a Loz an El Tiba bag full of clothes. Loz marched out of the shop feeling like he had won the pools. He nipped into the Pentagon and got his mum the chocolates and album and added a Status Quo album to it which he later gave to his dad.

'What did you buy then boy?' asked his dad.

Loz simply opened the El Tiba bag and showed his dad the goods.

'Well it's your money boy' was all he said and with that they drove home.

'Do you really think that we will get in' asked Theresa.

She and Loz walked hand in hand through the town centre on their way to the pictures. The town was virtually empty. It felt like it was recovering from a day's assault from greedy shoppers. Theresa had her hair crimped and Loz wasn't sure if he liked it. He didn't know if he was meant to say something or not. He decided to keep quiet.

'It should be alright, I have slipped into an eighteen before' he lied.

'They say it's a scary film so you'll have to sit close to me and hold my hand throughout the film.'

'Okay, I will but just don't natter through the film coz that really winds me up' he said.

'A Nightmare On Elm Street. It does sound scary doesn't it?' she said.

'It will be fine' He replied and squeezed her hand.

Every other shop window that they passed Loz glanced at his reflection. He felt like a peacock strutting its resplendent feathers dressed in his new trainers, trousers and kagool. Theresa caught him catching glimpses of himself.

'It's not going to rain you know' she teased 'But you look good in it.'

Loz felt good too. They continued to walk hand in hand down the hill that led to the cinema. They could see the queue was already coiled around the corner by the sports shop. They had no choice other than to join it and wait. Whilst they stood in the queue Loz told her the story of his back to back Star Wars experience and he pointed out the bakers opposite and recommended she buy a cream donut from there one day. He also told her about his trip to Yorkshire and about the custard slices.

The cinema doors eventually opened and within ten minutes Loz had purchased two tickets for the film with no questions asked. They walked up the carpeted steps to the room where the *Elm Street* film was to be played. Once inside they ignored the usherette holding her tray of ice creams and sweets and Theresa pushed Loz to the back row.

The other viewers piled into the cinema and dispersed amongst the seats. Some changed their minds and swopped a few more times before settling and others rattled their boxes of sweets and Popcorn. The lights lowered and a large Red curtain peeled back revealing the gigantic white screen. Voices hushed and the usherette guided a few late stragglers to their seats using her torch. Theresa clutched Loz's hand tightly and the trailer begun. They kissed throughout the entire trailer.

The trailers finished, the lights were turned up and the usherette reappeared selling her products. Loz pulled himself away from Theresa's lips and darted down to the usherette. He returned with a chocolate bar and a small tub of ice cream with two flat wooden spoons. They tucked into them and the main feature film began.

The film was shocking and horrific and Theresa couldn't watch it. Loz thought it was fantastic but disguised his fear. Sensing that the film was drawing to a close Theresa leaned over and started to kiss Loz's ear. It turned him on and made him shiver. He was still engrossed in the film though so Theresa slid her hand inside of his trousers and grabbed him. Loz felt the hairs on the back of his neck stand to attention along with his cock.

A few minutes later he groaned and Theresa's hand slowed to a halt. She then removed her hand and wiped her hand on the back of the seat in front. Loz wriggled in his seat as he felt the uncomfortable wetness turn cold in his pants. He then worried how he was going to exit the cinema with the damp patch showing through his trousers.

TIN SOLDIER

'Fucking hell!' screamed Robert looking Loz up and down.

Loz was dressed from head to toe in some of his brand new casual gear that he had bought with the money from his parents.

'Surprise, surprise.' Loz replied nervously.

Loz tightened his grip on Theresa's hand as they waited in the queue for the Trinity to open.

'So does this mean you're not a Mod anymore?' quizzed Robert, standing proud in his polo shirt and Loafers.

'That's right.'

'So what are you going to do with your old Moddy clobber and your records then?'

'Well I'll hold on to the clothes for now, I'm in no hurry to get rid of them. And the records, well just because I've turned into a casual it don't mean I suddenly dislike The Jam and Style Council' explained Loz.

'But that gear you have on is really expensive how comes you can afford it?'

'I got some money from my parents that they had been saving for me and I've also been fruit picking a few times and earnt some money.'

'Bloody hell, that was handy. I could do with some of that' said Robert.

The queue shuffled forward a few feet as the church doors creaked open.

'By the way I like the way you have cut slits into the bottom of your trousers. I have to say that does look good' observed Robert.

''Cheers' replied Loz thinking to himself wait until he sees the faded jeans with the frayed bottoms. Loz was itching to give them their debut. Theresa pushed Loz through the doorway and he paid their admission fee. Something by The Cure was playing and Loz screwed his nose up at it. Theresa gave him a peck on his cheek and ran off to greet some of her friends she had spotted who were dancing around their handbags. Loz and Robert walk over to the Mod's corner and Loz instantly felt out of place. Some of the Mod crowd quizzed him about his change of direction. Loz also noticed that some of them were mixing their clothes up a bit with a trainer here and a golf jumper there. Loz knew it was only a matter of time until before they would all be casuals.

Loz felt a body brush up beside him and he turned to see Gary and Reece standing there. He had not seen Reece since the Boxley Road episode or Gary since Yorkshire.

'Alright,' they said to one another.

'How's the fruit picking going?' asked Gary.

'It's a graft but the extra money helps, that's how I paid for some of this get up' said Loz.

'Yeah I can see you're well and truly kitted out now. You make a fine dresser mate.'

'Well I need the clothes because I'm intending to go football more often with Den and the others. How about you Reece, has your uncle taking you to anymore Ipswich games?'

'Yes he did and I got my photograph taken with Terry Butcher' announced Reece proudly.

'Yeah I'm hoping to do some away days. It would be something special to go with the Headhunters to Portman Road.'

'Are you going to keep the fruit picking going then to?' Gary asked.

'Yeah, but not every day. I've also got a job Saturday mornings holding a ladder and carrying buckets of water for some old bloke called Arthur. It puts a few extra quid in my pocket and will still give me plenty of time to go to footy.'

'Did you do anything about that Y.T.S thing?' asked Reece.

'No not yet. Anyway have you found a job yet?'

'Yep I've got a job that starts in two weeks. It's working for Top Man' said Reece.

They chatted for a bit longer before Gary and Reece went off to buy a can of fizzy drink. Loz watched them disappear into the darkness. He stood by himself and scanned the disco. Theresa had joined her friends dancing around their handbags. Loz stared at her swaying arse. Loz then watched Robert mingling and chatting with the Mod squad. He hoped that Robert would soon discard his Rude Boy look and join in with the casual affair. He then spotted Gary and Reece at the kiosk buying their drinks. He felt pleased that they had struck up a friendship. He just knew it would be a loyal and enduring relationship.

Loz looked at one familiar face and then another. Each face represented something about his teenage life. Each one of them had helped shape his personality to date. Life was far from perfect but he had nothing to regret so far. Just then Loz spotted Jed stroll through the Trinity doors. He was wearing his green flight jacket and had his crash helmet tucked under his arm. Following close behind him was Neil and his brother Paul. They looked drunk.

Loz had a nagging feeling that suggested something was different. He felt that he had grown up a little over the past few weeks. He felt like he was definitely leaving something behind. It was as if the transition from school boy to working boy was unfolding before him. He was the puppet but not the puppeteer. Loz looked at the faces in the crowd and wondered if they were feeling the same way as him.

Loz recalled the last significant change in his life. He had been alone in his bedroom and was overcome by an urge to look and touch his old childhood toy soldiers that he kept in a chocolates tin that had been a left over from one Christmas. The tin had been unopened for some time and hidden away under the bed.

Loz had dug the tin out and opened it. The tin and the soldiers had a unique familiar smell. It was a smell of his childhood. He had removed a handful of tiny soldiers and positioned them on the tin lid. Then suddenly it felt so wrong and so inappropriate.

The feeling had knocked him for six and he hastily poured the soldiers back into the tin, replaced the lid and pushed the tin back under the bed. That was last time he would ever look or touch them.

In that moment as Loz stared at the other youths he wondered how many other chocolate tins of soldiers and dolls were being hidden under beds. Loz felt like he was losing something and it frightened him but he also felt like he was discovering something and it thrilled him. The next moment *'Long hot summer'* began to play and a smile grew on his face

IT AINT NOTHING BUT A HOUSEPARTY

Week five of the school holidays was filled with three days fruit picking. His back ached but he sported a magnificent tan. Loz had also spent one day in London with his friend Mark whom he knew from school. They had not seen each other since the last school day. The two chums had caught the train to London where Mark was going to visit his Nan before they went exploring in the city. His Nan lived by herself in Crystal Palace.

On the train to London Mark had explained that when he was younger he used to spend most school summer holidays with his Nan and since departed Granddad. He spoke endearingly about those days and Loz enjoyed listening to Mark's recollections. They had reached Mark's Nans terrace house just before lunch time. She had fed them with sandwiches and Swiss roll before they set off to soak up the sights and smells of the city.

On the way to the bus stop they took a shortcut through a kid's playground. There was a large dug out area that Mark explained used to be a paddling pool. A few feet away there was another hole that used to be the sand pit. Both were empty. The two boys gaped at the holes wondering where the water and sand had gone. Just then an old man wearing a tank top and smoking a pipe sided up to them. He blew smoke in their faces then told them the story of the missing sand and water. He informed them that the council had needed to remove the sand and water because foolish and dangerous people kept leaving broken glass in the paddling pool and sand pit. The old man looked sad as he told them the stories of injured children. He added that one of his grandchildren had been on the injured children and then he hobbled away cursing the modern world. The two boys were left disturbed after this encounter.

They caught the bus to Piccadilly Circus and spent the next few hours simply strolling about. The only shop they visited was Lillywhites where Loz bought a beige golf jumper in the sale. He paid fifty pounds for it even though it was a size to big. On the bus back to Mark's Nans Loz left the jumper on the bus and Mark had to run after it. He eventually flagged the bus driver down and retrieved the jumper. Loz was eternally grateful to Mark after that.

It was now Friday and Loz had a couple of hours spare before he was due to meet Theresa. They were heading off to a house party that evening. The party was being held at one of Theresa's friend's homes whose parents had gone away for the weekend. Loz didn't really like house parties and was only going because Theresa wanted him to.

Loz didn't have good memories of house parties. A year earlier his own parents had gone away for the weekend. His parents had left his younger brother with his Nan but had trusted his sister and him to look after the house. Loz's sister had breached their parents trust and had organised a party at their home. Loz's friends turned up dressed in the best Ra Ra skirts and their boyfriends had followed. The first couple of hours had been okay. Nothing had been spilt or broken. Then at ten o clock a gang of notorious Punks showed up. Somehow they had got wind of the house party. Loz's sister then battled to get rid of them. It had been a frightening experience. Fortunately the party passed on okay with nothing being damaged or stolen and Loz's parents were none the wiser.

So although Loz felt house parties was a risky business he was going to one because of Theresa. He just hoped it would be an uneventful evening and he would still get to screw her at the end. To pass the spare time Loz collected his sketch pad and pencils together and sat on his bed. He picked out the single cover to The Jam's *'Bitterest Pill'* and decided to copy it. Quietly in the background he played The Jam's *'Gift'* album.

Loz rested the sketch pad on his knees and began by drawing the arch window with the shaft of light coming through it. Loz concentrated and took his time. His anxieties switched off as he got deeper into the sketching. It felt good drawing the stone bricks of the prison cell walls. He was copying the sleeve design perfectly. It had feel and atmosphere in it. The drawing took longer than he anticipated and he had to stop before he could complete it. He placed the pad and pencils carefully under his bed.

Loz picked some items of clothing out of the wardrobe and got dressed. He drenched himself in Mandate aftershave, turned off the record and went down stairs to the kitchen. The remaining last slice of his mum's homemade bakewell tart sat on a plate. He picked it up and scoffed it. His mum made the best bakewell tarts in the world. They were much better than Mr Kiplins he told himself.

Loz was still dusting off the crumbs of the cake when he left the house waving goodbye to his parents who were watching *Emmerdale*. The irritating theme music was playing so Loz made a sharp exit. Loz had phoned Gary, Robert and Reece earlier in the day and had told them all to meet him outside the Howard Wardell. From there they would go and meet Theresa and then head off to the party together. This way they would all ensure getting into the party because they would be with Theresa.

Robert was crouched down with his back against the exterior wall of the Howard Wardell. Gary and Reece had not arrived yet.

'Alright Loz, I'm glad you're early' he said.

'Why is that?' asked Loz.

'Do you remember Nip's dad complaining that somebody had stolen the chairs from outside the pub. Well, I think I know where they are. I took the shortcut through the alley in Waterloo Street on the way here and the house at the very end has the same plastic white chairs that Nip's dad had. What do you reckon?'

'Could be' said Loz checking his watch 'Look we have some time before Gary and Reece show up so let's nip round the pub and mention it to Nips dad'.

With that they walked up the street to the pub. Nip's dad was behind the bar drying pint glasses. Loz explained why they were there and Robert described the plastic chairs.

'Right, I'll get Nip and the dog and you can show me where they are' he roared.

The next thing Loz knew he, Robert, Nip and Nips dad plus the Alsatian dog were marching through the alley towards Waterloo Street. Robert pointed to the house where a man was supping a can of beer whilst sitting on one of the plastic chairs. Nips dad instantly recognised the chairs as being his property and confronted the man. The dog growled and barked and the man owned up to the theft.

Five minutes later Nip and Loz were carrying the plastic chairs back to the pub. Nips dad thanked them and poured some beer down their throats before Loz and Robert shot off to go and meet Gary and Reece.

On their arrival at the party they dived onto the table of grub which consisted of sausage rolls, crisps and biscuits. Robert had 'borrowed' a bottle of Whiskey from his dad's stash and was filling small plastic cups up with it for his mates. Loz sipped his slowly. He still hadn't acquired a taste for the fiery water. There was already a group swelling of boys and girls of every tribe. Peroxide hair and flicks mingled together.

Loz spotted a space on the host's sofa and flopped down onto it. It smelt of dog hair and cigarette smoke. He observed Theresa conversing with her friends. He thought she looked gorgeous. He was discovering new things about her that was increasing his attraction to her all the time. He was enjoying the experience of falling in love for the first time.

Theresa must have felt Loz's eyes pulling her towards him and she turned to look at him. They exchanged a knowing smile and then she left her friends and went to sit on his lap. Theresa kissed Loz passionately until he had to push her away to gasp for some air. They giggled and then braced themselves for another round of kissing. However Robert plonked himself down on the sofa next to them and splashed whiskey over them.

'Hey Theresa, what do you think the chances are for me and your mate Debbie getting it on?'

Theresa looked at him as if he had insulted her. 'Getting it on' she said 'I think somebodies been watching too much *Miami Vice*.'

'What?' said a confused and startled Robert.

Loz intervened 'Theresa's only joking mate. She'll have a word with her won't you?'

Theresa looked at Loz and then at Robert.

'Yes I'll have a word with her later, but I can't promise you anything, I know she's keen on someone else.'

'Who'? asked Robert.

'I can't say. Look, just leave it with me.'

'Alright, cheers, but put a good word in yeah' Robert pleaded.

'Yes okay, now clear off will you mate' said Loz.

Robert huffed and slowly climbed off of the sofa. Theresa and Loz laughed and then returned to their snog. One of the host's older brothers had assumed control of the record player and had strung a continued list of New Romantic songs together. The only song he liked was one by Haircut 100. Loz felt okay hiding underneath Theresa on the sofa.

Before nine o' clock had arrived a bunch of girls had already participated in a vomiting session in the garden. They had drunk too much red wine and the kitchen was left smelling of puke. One of the sick girls staggered to the sofa which Loz and Theresa had not budged from and flopped herself down onto it and curled up into a ball. The waft of vomit was unbearable. The girl also had traces of puke in her matted perm her. One thing Loz could not stand was sick. He couldn't watch anybody be sick and he certainly couldn't tolerate the stench of it.

Loz grabbed Theresa's hand and led her away from the sofa to another room. As they passed the stairs they spotted the host disappearing upstairs with a Nik Kershaw look alike. Theresa grabbed a handful of crisps and offered some to Loz. He refused, there was no way he could stomach any food after the sick girl.

'Alright Loz or should I say Top Boy.'

Loz spun around recognising the voice. It was Den standing tall and proud in a yellow and blue argyle pattern jumper and jumbo cords. Loz was pleased to see him. They had not seen or spoken to each other since their day out in Chelsea a couple of weeks earlier.

'Alright Den, good to see you. Have you been back to the Bridge yet?'

'Not the Bridge but Mark, Malc, Gus and me went for an away day to Spurs. We ran them

all over their shit hole of a ground. That whole area of White Hart Lane is a dump' replied Den puffing his chest out.

'Did you swing by Stuarts? Did you get anything?' asked Loz.

'No I haven't been back to Stuarts but I did pop over to El Tiba's. I bought myself a really nice Gabicci jumper'.

'I did what you suggested actually and also went to El Tiba's. It's where I bought these bits from.'

'I can see. You look good mate.'

Loz felt ten feet tall after Den's acknowledgement and comments. Theresa sqeezed his hand and it hurt.

'Oh, yeah, by the way this is Theresa' introduced Loz.

'Nice to meet you Theresa. Is this your bird then mate?'

Loz thought for a moment. He had not considered that Theresa and he were officially boyfriend and girlfriend yet. He then announced.

'Yes Den, this is my bird.'

126

'Nice one Loz she's a cracker, you have done alright for yourself. Look I'm going to sort myself out a drink so I'll see you later yea. And I'll chat to you about our next home game with Ipswich.'

'Right, okay, cheers' said Loz.

Den disappeared into the kitchen. Loz could see that Theresa was impressed that her new boyfriend knew one of the faces. She also thanked him for making their relationship official. Loz said she could thank him later on that evening and he poured some more whiskey into her cup.

An eclectic mix of records then graced the party. Duran Duran followed The Style Council and that followed Level 42. Loz and Theresa had found another sofa to perch themselves on and they stuck their tongues down the others throat.

They were still licking each other's tonsils when the sound of commotion disturbed them. The racket was coming from the hall way area of the house. Loz pulled his tongue out and wiped his mouth with his jumper sleeve before gently sliding Theresa off of him and standing up. A couple of people dashed past him heading in the direction of the shouts and screams. Loz went to investigate. Just as he reached the hall way he heard somebody cry out 'Skinheads'.

Loz was overcome with a sense of dread. He felt a sick sensation in his stomach and he started to sweat as he realized that Webby, Walshy and their skinhead gang had sniffed them out to execute their revenge. The hallway had around a dozen bodies trying to block the way so that the Skinheads could not enter. Their resistance was futile. Loz could see the fierce expressions on the faces of the Skinheads. Walshy and Simmons had one boy up against the wall whilst punching his face. Webby held another by the throat whilst another Skinhead used the boy's body for his punch bag practice. Other hard looking Skinheads dressed in their Crombies and boots lashed out at others trying to defend themselves.

The Skinhead's blurry eyes were full of rage and determination. The females in the party screamed and pleaded for the fighting to stop. A wall mirror in the hall way crashed to the floor knocking off a ceramic vase on its way down. More Skinheads piled through the door and pushed their opponents back into the front room. The hostess and her lover stood at the top of the stairs in tears. Theresa fled to the dining room with some of her friends. They were all crying.

The front room became a mass of brawling bodies. The continual sound of thuds and slaps filled the air. Furniture was knocked over and glass ornaments smashed. Loz stumbled over a body that had fallen on the floor in front of him. He looked down and saw that it was Gary. He had a gash on his head and blood trickled down his face. Loz helped him back to his feet before he was pushed over himself. Loz fell back onto his bottom and just in the nick of time saw an airwear boot heading towards his face. Loz dodged the boot and instead of kicking him it kicked the record player. The record on the deck went flying into the air and the record player collapsed onto the floor. The music ended.

The Skinhead who had tried to kick Loz but had missed lifted his boot for another attempt and was about to stamp down when Robert appeared and landed a punch onto the bonehead's skull. He stumbled and fell into a group of fighting youths who then turned their attention on him. Robert helped Loz to his feet. As Loz climbed to his feet he noticed Den having a one on one box with Simmons. Spit, blood and sweat sprayed everywhere.

Gary was joined by Reece and they jumped onto a Skinhead pushing him to the floor. Den was about to join in when suddenly he saw that Den was needing to fight off both Webby and Walshy. The two Skinhead aggressors raged war onto Den's body and he scrambled to protect his face and stomach. The skins were about to drag Den to the floor so without a second thought Loz hurled himself into the affray. He punched Webby on the side of the face and heard the sound of its impact. Surely one or two teeth had been shattered. Webby turned to look at the person who had punched him and Loz struck again punching him on the nose. Loz heard the Skinheads nose break. Webby stumbled over a chair and collapsed into a heap on the floor holding his nose.

Den had now overcome Walshy and had him curled up into a ball on the floor where he repeatedly stamped on him. Loz pulled Den away and stepped back just in time to see another skin put his boot through the television screen. There were bits of broken furniture all over the floor. Loz could hear the girls in the dining room still screaming and crying and then he heard the sound of glass smashing.

Den heard it to and looked at Loz. Standing behind Loz was Webby clutching a broken wine bottle in his hand. The Skinhead's bloody face sneered at them. Den jumped onto Webby and they pushed and pulled each other all the way out into the hall. Loz felt a cold wet trickle on his neck. He put his hand onto it and then looked at his hand. Next his version went blurry and he passed out.

Loz came around with his head laying on Theresa's lap. As he regained his focus he could see that she had tears in her eyes. Theresa lovingly stroked his cheek. Loz realized that he felt nauseous and wanted to be sick. He had never experienced a headache like the one he had. Loz sensed that other people crowded around him. He didn't like the attention he was getting.

'Take your time, there's no rush' whispered Theresa smiling down into his face. She dabbed the back of his head again with a tea towel. The tea towel felt cold and damp. It reminded him of the last sensation he felt before passing out.

'Is my head still bleeding? What happened? Am I okay?' he blurted.

'It's stopped bleeding don't worry there's an ambulance on the way,' said Theresa.

'Ambulance!' yelled Loz and tried to sit up. His head hurt even more.

'Stay still, the ambulance people will check your head for you. They will look to see if there are any bits of wine bottle stuck in there.'

Loz laid back on the floor. The thought of having pieces of glass wedged in his skull frightened him. He turned his head to the side and saw the destruction in the front room. The television lay in a heap on the floor with its shattered screen. Nearly every piece of furniture was toppled over and ornaments and vases lay scattered and broken on shelves.

'Where are Webby and the other skins?' asked Loz.

'They have gone. After they saw you collapse on the floor they ran off. Den, Gary and the rest of your mates have run after them. I don't know where they have gone.'

'How long was I unconscious for?'

'Only a couple of minutes. I called the ambulance as I saw you get hit with the bottle.'

Theresa was then pushed aside and two ambulance men stared down at him. They were still treating Loz when a policeman tried asking Loz some questions.

'So who did this son?' asked the fat copper.

Loz shrugged his shoulders.

'Do you know their names?' asked the other.

Again Loz said nothing and realizing that Loz was not going to spill the beans let alone press any charges they gave up. The ambulance men cleaned Loz's head up and assured him that no pieces of glass were stuck in his scalp. Loz sighed. Five minutes later both the ambulance men and the Police officers left.

Loz had been moved to a chair and Theresa knelt down in front of him. Her friends and the hostess started to tidy up. Theresa helped Loz to his feet and said she would walk him home. They left the war zone after saying their goodbyes and offering apologies.

Loz's body ached. He felt that he had bruises on his back and face. His head still ached and was sore. Theresa held his hand tightly as they walked through the streets towards Loz's house. When they reached the top of Loz's street they stopped for a final rest. Loz plonked himself down on the steps of the Post Office and Theresa sat beside him. The night sky was like a dark blanket with pin holes in it where the light from the next galaxy shone through. There was no breeze and the surrounding houses were still and quiet. Loz and Theresa sat in silence for a few moments before Theresa asked what the building site opposite the Post Office was for.

'My dad said they are going to build eight small houses on the site.'

'Really, can they get eight houses on there? It doesn't look bigger enough for more than three at the most.'

'Like I say they will only be small' said Loz.

'What used to be there?' asked Theresa.

'It used to be a dump. It was one of the last left over bomb sites from the war. Throughout all my growing up years we used to play in there. It seemed like a jungle when we were kids. It's shrunk as I've got older. I remember me and my next door neighbour sneaked in there one day and found a camp that my neighbour's older brother and his mates had built out of things they found around the dump. Inside the camp they had an old lorry inner tube, a table made out of stones and a few candles had been wedged in the cracks. I recall it felt creepy and I didn't want to crawl inside. I did and once inside I couldn't wait to get out. I was also scared that my neighbour's older brother might catch us in their camp.'

'Let's go and take a look around?' said Theresa.

Loz tried to resist but Theresa was adamant that she wanted to explore so he led her to the building site. The boundary had been marked with a metal fence but Loz had no trouble pulling two parts of it open. He squeezed through the gap and Theresa followed.

It was quiet inside the site. Loz perched himself on the edge of a cement mixer and Theresa continued to look explore. She leaned through windows which were still waiting for the glass to be installed and poked her head through doorways and then she disappeared. Loz waited but she didn't return. He quietly called out her name but she didn't reply.

Loz walked off into the darkness in search of her. He went in and out of three houses but there was no sign of her. Then suddenly he felt a warm pair of hands cover his eyes. 'Boo' she whispered and then swung him around. Theresa had removed her sweatshirt and stood topless in front of him. She kissed him gently and guided his hand towards her breast. Loz squeezed her tit and she let out a whimpering sound.

Theresa then unzipped his trousers and slid her hand down into his pants. All his aches and pains receded. He grabbed her tightly and kissed her passionately on her neck. They fell to the dusty floor and landed on some canvas tarpaulin. They raced to undress each other and before long both lay naked holding one another. Suddenly Theresa jumped as she heard a rustle behind her. Loz sat up and stared into the darkness wondering what could of made the noise. 'Sshh' he said and they waited.

They heard the rustle again and then a Fox poked its nose through the doorway. The animal looked directly at the two naked bodies and scampered away. Loz and Theresa laughed and then made love to each other.

SOLID BOND IN YOUR HEART

Loz awoke to the sound of ruffling and things being moved around on his bedside table. His mum was clearing a space so that she could put the steaming hot mug of tea down that she had made for him. Loz sat up and rubbed the sleep from his eyes. His mum then sat on the edge of his bed and looked at him. Loz thought she would burst into tears at any moment.

'How are you feeling?' She asked holding back the tears.

'Mum I'm ok now. It's been two days. You can stop bringing me tea up every morning, I really am fine.'

'Okay. Your dad and me are going down to the market do you want to come?' she said.

'No thanks. I'm going to pop into the job centre today to see if there is anything new in there. The fruit picking job has finished now.'

'There's a letter down stairs for you and it looks official, perhaps that's the Youth Training Scheme thingy.'

'Might be, they did say my application would take a few weeks to be processed.'

'Now you're sure you don't want to come to the market? We may even nip over to Nanny Courts later to so if we do we will bring you some of her bread back. I've got a list of things to do and people to visit. I don't know Loz it feels like the long hot summer just passed me by.'

It doesn't feel like that to me Loz thought to himself as his mum left his bedroom. Loz sipped his sweet tea and stared out of his sky light. He couldn't spot a single cloud in the sky. One of his earliest memories returned. He could of only been four or five. It was summertime and he lay in his bed in the house he lived in before moving to where he was now. Loz remembered staying awake listening to the older children playing in the street outside. He wished he could have been with them and then he fell to sleep. For some unbeknown reason that memory had lodged itself in Loz's mind.

Loz shook the memory away and got out of bed. He slipped on a pair of cords and tee shirt and went downstairs to the kitchen. His parents had already left and the house was empty. No doubt his younger brother was with his Nan and his sister was probably at work. She just started a new job working in the Royal Mail restaurant. The posties loved her.

Loz fetched the biscuit tin and pulled out two custard creams which he gobbled quickly. He then went over to the kitchen window and saw that his brother must have been playing swing ball earlier. He had left it up in the garden. He then sat at the kitchen table and gently pressed the wound on the back of his head. It was still sore but he knew it would heal soon. His mum had left the brown letter on the table for him and he tore it open. Loz read the letter and smiled. It was from the Y.T.S. They were offering him the position of trainee paint sprayer and panel beater at Duttons. This will please Mum he thought to himself. He tried to feel more excited but it was hard, he was only going to be getting paid twenty seven pounds and fifty pence. He left the letter on the table and returned to his bedroom.

Something seemed different and he found himself standing in the middle of his bedroom. He looked at all the walls with their collections of posters of The Jam, The Who, scooters and other clippings from the *New Musical Express, Sounds* and *Melody Maker* on them. They looked dated to him. Some of them had been on his bedroom walls for three or more years. Loz decided it was time for them to come down and one by one he removed them and made a pile of them which he then pushed under his bed. The only picture he left on the wall was the sketch he had drawn of the *'Ever changing moods'* single sleeve.

Next Loz looked at his wardrobe. There were two piles of different clothes. He spent the next few minutes putting all his Sta-prest, shirts and other Moddy togs into a bin liner and shoved them under his bed along with the posters. He then hung all his new designer sportswear clothes neatly in the wardrobe. Loz then sorted out his shoes and trainers separating them out into two piles. Loafers, brogues and Jam shoes to the left and all his new trainers to the right. He bagged up his Mod shoes and pushed them under the bed as well. Next he peered down at his record collection and smiled. The records were just fine as they were.

Loz tied the laces on his Wimbledon's and left the house. He chose to take a route to town that he rarely used. As he walked past the small terrace houses he took time to look at them in a way he had not looked before. He admired their defiance because they had withstood the bombs and bullets from the 'Battle of Britain' that had raged above them forty years earlier. Loz wondered who lived in the houses now. He wondered what their lives were like, what jobs they done and how long they had lived in them. Each and every one of them was clean and tidy and Loz felt respectful.

Loz crossed the road near the entrance to the Prison and slipped through a graveyard. The church that used to be there had long since disappeared and been turned into a car park. He passed through another alley and found himself amongst throngs of shoppers darting this way and that. Loz looked through the window of the store and remembered the day Neil and Paul had stolen the music cassettes. He then reminded himself that he had not played the Dexy's *'Searching for the young soul rebels'* tape yet and would need to do so soon.

Loz marched to the job centre and walked inside. He walked straight over to a woman wearing glasses who was sitting behind a desk with a plaque on it that said 'Here to help'. She wore an outfit that Loz had only ever seen on *Dallas*. Loz pulled out the grey plastic bucket chair and sat down in it thinking to himself that the miserable looking woman did not have a clue about style. The woman continued to do something with the computer in front of her and made no attempt to welcome her customer.

Loz waited patiently, then sniffed, then coughed in an attempt to get her attention. She looked over her glasses at him and frowned.

'I'll be with you in a minute' she said coldly.

Another minute passed and then she asked Loz if she could be of assistance.

'I'm looking for a job' said Loz.

'Your name, age and address please,' she said.

'Lawrence Richard Stead, sixth of June nineteen seventy.'

'Thank you. Do you have some idea of the kind of employment that you want or are skilled in?'

Loz paused for a moment thinking that neither applied.

'I have been offered a position on the Y.T.S'.

'Ah, that's very good news' she returned.

'Well yes and no really. The training is good but the pay is a bit, well, you know, shit.'

The woman hissed at him and shuffled in her seat before frowning at him again. She told him to wait in the chair whilst she walked over to the notice boards and collected a few job cards. When she returned she placed them in a row on the table. She dealt with each card one at a time. There was one for the Army, the Navy and the Air force, a factory worker and a mechanic.

'Are any of these of any interest?' she asked.

Loz screwed his nose up.

'They are not really me' he said.

'And what would be you?'

Loz screwed his nose up again, arose from out of the chair and left the job centre. He resigned himself to accepting the Y.T.S position. Before heading off to the hut Loz decided he would swing by the Wander Inn for a cup of tea. Instead of turning left and climbing up Gabriels Hill he turned left and took the route that passed the art deco building opposite the Magistrates Courts. He walked parallel with the river and watched a few kids dangling their fishing rods into it. The best they will get will be pike he thought to himself.

He then crossed the road and opened the door of the café. Immediately the smell of bacon and coffee assaulted him. Den was sitting at the table at the rear with Mark and waved to him. Loz tilted his head back and walked over to join them.

'Alright Loz, how's your swede?' laughed Den.

'Better than it was a few days ago. It fucking hurt the following morning' replied Loz.

'What a night that turned out to be eh' said Den.

'Theresa told me that you lot chased the Boneheads away after they laid me out. Where did you go? What happened?'

'We did chase them and me a few others caught up with Webby and Walshy and we gave them a right pasting. Anyway it's all sorted now. I've seen Webby since and it's been agreed that that is it for now and a line has been drawn under it all. I think he was shitting himself in case you or someone has given the Old Bill their names. Webby has done Borstal in the past so he wouldn't look good in court. So it's done and spread the word to your mates alright.'

'Fucking hell, that's a relief and good to know, I really didn't fancy having to look over my shoulder all the bloody time' sighed Loz.

'Yeah so look on the bright side' said Mark 'All of this has done your reputation a world of good.'

The café waitress came over and took Loz's order of a cup of tea. They didn't normally bother but had on this occasion because the café was almost empty.

'What are you doing Friday night?' asked Den.

'I have got plans sorry.'

'No worries, it's just that The Prisoners are playing again over in Strood and we are planning to go over. Next time eh.'

'Yeah, next time. I can't get out of Friday night Theresa wants me to go with her to this new disco for under eighteens at the Kent Hall so I had better go.'

'Yes mate you go. Keep in her good books, she is a cracker you know, you did alright there.'

It pleased Loz that Den had been impressed with Theresa. The waitress returned with the cup of tea and the bill. Loz poured two spoonfuls of sugar in the tea and gulped it down. The three of them then finished their teas together and chatted about football and fashion.

Loz arrived home just in time for dinner. His mum had made a Shepherd's pie. The whole family gathered around the kitchen table. The three kids sat in their adopted seats with their backs to the kitchen wall whilst Loz's mum and dad sat on the bench opposite. Loz's mum tried to fuss over his injuries again but he shook her off. She placed five plates full of wonderfully smelling Shepherd's pie onto the table. Loz noticed that he had been given an extra portion of his favourite crusty bit from the top of the pie. One after the other they poured steaming hot gravy onto their meals and tucked in.

'How's the job going?' Loz asked his sister civilly.

'Yes it is okay. It's mostly just serving the postmen' she answered.

'Have you been chatted up yet?'

'Yes I have and I'm going out Friday with a postman called Phil. He plays guitar. Anyway how is it going with THERESA?'

'Who is Theresa?' said Loz's mum.

'Loz has a girlfriend mum, didn't you know, hasn't he told you yet?'

'No he hasn't. So who is she and when are going to introduce us to her?'

Loz resigned himself to telling his mum that Theresa and he had known each other for a long time and had been seeing each other for a couple of weeks. He said he would bring her around the house soon and introduce her then. Loz's sister was about to launch into another wind up but Loz's dad intervened.

'What are you doing Sunday Loz?' asked his dad.

'Erm, not sure, why?'

'I'm going to a boot fair in Ditton first thing if you want to come, you never know you might find some records. Then at ten there is another meeting of the Archaeological group down that site behind the Royal Mail building. People will have their metal detectors and will be searching for Roman coins again. So if you want to come just make sure you are up on time.'

Loz occasionally accompanied his dad on the metal detector explorations. Loz had always been attracted to things of an ancient or historical nature. He had grown up loving to flick through his dads books on the Egyptians or the Romans. His sister or younger brother had not shown much interest so it pleased his dad that Loz had.

It had been the same with sport. Throughout Loz's growing up years his dad had participated in most sports. His dad was forever joining the various clubs and teams within the Royal Mail. There had been snooker, cricket, and dominoes. Loz had particularly enjoyed going with his dad to the cricket matches. He especially liked the cheese and cucumber sandwiches and coconut cakes that used to get served up. Cheese and cucumber sandwiches always reminded Loz of those cricket expeditions.

One by one plates of Shepherd's pie were finished off and one by one Loz's mum stacked the empty plates beside the sink. She then went over to the fridge and produced one of her home made lemon meringue pies. The after's was one of Loz's mums specialities and adored by the family. Loz ravished his bowls worth.

'Did you read the letter mum?' Loz asked.

'Yes, it's good news. Are you going to accept it?'

'Yes, I think I will' he replied.

'Good. When you do I will want five pounds boarding money' she added.

'What?' cried Loz.

'Five pounds keep, just like your sister has to pay.'

'But she earns more than me working down the Royal Mail restaurant.'

'Five pounds!'

Loz's sister and brother smirked. His dad had not been paying attention because he had started doing the washing up. It was agreed that it was Loz's younger brothers turn to do the washing up so Loz and his sister exited the kitchen and retreated to their bedrooms.

'Fucking stinks in there with all that perfume and hair spray mixed together'. Loz shouted as he passed his sister's room. She didn't reply but slammed the door. Once in his bedroom he changed his clothes and splashed some Mandate around his chin. He noticed he had a few more whiskers forming. That cheered him up.

He grabbed one of his tracksuit tops and left the house heading for Theresa's. It had been arranged that he would be meeting Theresa's parents for the first time and he felt nervous. He walked slowly to her house. It was a modern three story house tucked away at the end of a close. Loz rang the doorbell and waited. Through the stained glass window in the door he identified Theresa bounce up to the door. She opened it and was grinning like a Cheshire cat. Theresa pulled himself gave him a quick peck on the lips and told him to follow her.

The house had a modern feel to it. Thick wool carpet in the passage way and a grandfather clock dominated the wall near the stair way. Loz thought the house smelt of fish and chips. He assumed that's what they must have had for their tea. Theresa ushered Loz towards the front room. Her parents were sitting on a large cream leather sofa watching *Crossroads*. Theresa's mum smiled politely and introduced herself. Her dad looked at him suspiciously. Loz shuffled on the spot and introduced himself in his best Queens English but he could see that Theresa's dad could see through it.

Theresa informed her parents that Loz had been accepted a Y.T.S. position and would starting his new training soon. Her dad seemed unimpressed so Loz informed them that the position was at Duttons. Loz felt he had not scored any points with Theresa's dad as she led him upstairs to her bedroom.

'My mum and dad like you' Theresa assured, but Loz didn't believe her. Once inside her bedroom Loz was able to relax. Theresa switched on a small bedside lamp and pulled the curtains closed. Theresa's bedroom was painted a pale pink and it had large posters of Wham and ABC on the walls. The room smelt the same as his sisters. She had a single size bed with purple bed sheets. Theresa turned up the radio and pushed Loz onto her bed. He tried to scramble away from her.

'What are you doing?' He said 'We can't snog in your bedroom with your dad and mum downstairs.'

'Don't worry about them, they cannot hear anything.'

'But what if your dad walks in on us? He will fucking kill me.'

'Relax, they trust me. They are not going to disturb us. Just remember you're not the first boyfriend I have brought home.'

Theresa gave Loz a cheeky wink and then jumped on him again. They kissed and Loz kept one eye on the door. They continued to kiss for a few more minutes and Loz calmed down a little.

They spent the next two hours pleasuring each other and then Loz announced that it was time for him to leave. They both sorted themselves out and Theresa led him back downstairs and back into the front room so that he could say goodnight to her parents. Theresa's mum looked up from watching the nine o clock news and her dad looked up from reading his newspaper. He again looked at Loz suspiciously. Loz felt like sending him a cheeky 'you know what I've been doing to your daughter' wink but decided it would not be prudent to do so. He simply said goodnight and left.

The next few days dragged for Loz. He attended the Howard Wardell only once. He had only gone to remove himself from the tension left in the house after an argument between his dad and his sister. They whole family had retreated to the front room after scoffing plates of fish and chips. They were laughing at *Harold Lloyd* on the telly. Loz's dad has informed his children for the hundredth time that Harold had done all his own stunts. The first few times Loz had heard this he had genuinely been impressed, but now, he could not give a shit.

All was going okay and Loz's mum even shared a box of mint chocolates with everybody. Then Loz's sister asked if she could stay out on the forthcoming Friday night until eleven o' clock. Loz's dad had said no, ten was the curfew time. Loz's sister reacted by arguing that Loz was allowed to stay out later then her. She tried to argue the point that her brother had always been allowed to stay out later and it was simply not fair, especially as she was the eldest. Loz's dad still refused and still evaded providing a reason for this arrangement.

Over the years Loz had sometimes teased his sister on this matter but he no longer could be arsed to get involved. The argument escalated and eventually Loz's sister stormed off to her bedroom and slammed the door hard behind her. His dad disappeared to the kitchen to get some peace and smoke a roll up and Loz headed off to the youth club leaving his mum and brother to munch on the chocolates.

The only other memorable event of that particular night was watching his friend Steve run around the Howard Wardell with his White shirt poking out through his unzipped sta-prest pretending that it was his cock hanging out. Steve had been doing this for most of the secondary school years. Loz presumed the joke would continue until the day his school mate would 'kick the bucket'. The other was a story that Nip retold about a girl that one of the pubs locals had told him. The man had just returned from working up in Wigan. Whilst working up there he and his work mates had attended the Wigan Casino soul club anniversary party. During the night he had fallen for and chatted up one of the soul girls. The man had then told the locals in Nip's dad pub that the girl was a true Northern Soulie saying all she done was 'think soul, slept soul, dreamed soul and danced soul, but when I asked if she took it up the arsehole she punched me'. The story made everyone laugh.

On returning home after the Howard Wardell Loz found everybody in the house asleep in their beds. Loz was not tired enough and didn't relish the thought of staring up at the ceiling for the next three hours whilst trying to get to sleep. Instead he made himself a mug of Horlicks and switched the television on. After he had flicked through all four channels he returned to BBC2 to watch the *Hammer House Of Horrors* film that had already started. The music was chilling and Loz curled up on the settee. The film was rubbish and involved some haunted house that spurted gallons of thick red blood out of pipes and walls. Loz had a nightmare that night and woke up in the morning still feeling the effects of it. Only a large bowl of 'Frosties' and a sweet tea helped shake off the bad feeling.

The day after the youth club and the Hammer film Loz had visited Reece. Loz was intrigued to hear more of Reece's records, especially the ones by The Doors and The Velvet Underground. Loz spent most of the day with Reece drinking his tea and eating his biscuits. Reece introduced him to *'Transformer'* by Lou Reed, *'Ziggy Stardust'* by Bowie, *'The Soft Parade'* by The Doors and dozens of other albums by The Velvet Underground, Japan, Joy Division and The Smiths. Loz liked some of the records but abhorred others. He could not make head or tails of The Smiths who had recently exploded onto the pop charts and a million kid's hearts.

On one of the days Loz awoke not feeling very well. He blamed The Smiths. It took him a while to pull himself out of bed. He wondered if it was just a dose of hayfever but nonetheless decided to stay home for the day. Theresa phoned him at lunch time wanting to know if he had time to pop round to hers to 'look at some old photographs'.

Loz was tempted but complained about not feeling very well so Theresa visited him instead. He only had a few old photographs to impress her with. One was of him when he was five bashing away on a plastic snare drum in his Nan's garden, another was of him, his sister and his brother splashing around in swimsuits in a big metal bath in the garden of their former house and one other photograph of Loz in a Red Indian outfit.

Loz also retold the story of the outfit. There had been some event at his Primary school Saint Pauls. For the event all the children were required to dress up as either Cowboys or Indians. Even dirty poor old Pottsy turned up looking like John Wayne. Loz went to school that day in an outfit that his mum had made. It included a headdress with dozens of Pigeon feathers attached to it, a suede waist coat and a pair of old jeans that his mum attached more Pigeon feathers to.

Loz and his class had been practicing a dance routine that involved going around and around a paper mache totem pole. All the mums had been invited to witness the event and stood around the playground looking bored but proud of their costume creations. Whilst Loz got dizzy going round and around his outfit gradually started to fall apart. Several times his mum rushed forward to make speedy repairs but in the end it was to no avail. The outfit had started off looking good but had deteriorated into a disaster zone. Loz didn't really care, he was just glad his mum had made the effort.

Loz told Theresa that it was the last outfit he ever allowed his mum to make for him. He added though that his Nan had been a bit nifty with the knitting needles and once made him a woollen jumper that he had designed himself. It was his attempt at something similar to what Paul Weller wore on the cover of the *'This is the Modern world'* album. The jumper was jet Black with a two White arrows. One arrow pointed up the other down. Loz told Theresa the jumper shrunk in the wash a few months after it was completed.

Theresa had enjoyed looking at Loz's photographs. She also enjoyed stroking the inside of his thigh. Once the photographs and stories had finished she jumped onto Loz, who had perked up a little. However in her launching herself at him she accidently kicked the glass door on the familys hi-fi system. The door smashed and scattered glass over a five foot radius. Loz's hardened prick drooped as he heard the sound of shattering glass as they both done their best to collect all the pieces of glass loz dreaded having to explain to his mum and dad how it had happened.

Friday night eventually crept up on Loz and he set off to meet Theresa who he had not seen or spoken to since the glass door incident. She had not been avoiding Loz but she had been avoiding his parents. Loz met Theresa outside the mini-market opposite the Dog pub. They kissed and hugged in full view of the passing traffic. They didn't care. A few minutes later Robert, Gary and Reece joined them. The group strolled to the children's playground near the Howard Wardell. Before they had chance to jump over the wall Dave ran out of the youth club and asked them if they were going inside because he had arranged another disco in the dungeons below. Robert had gently informed him that they had other plans. They were going to check out the opening of a new under eighteens disco at the Kent Hall. Dave plodded off looking rejected. Loz felt sorry for him and then jumped over the wall with the others.

Paul and Neil and several other kids were waiting in the playground. They had decided to go to the new disco mobhanded. The disco was open to everyone and anyone under eighteen years old in the town. So unlike the Howard Wardell or the Trinity discos where everybody seemed to know everybody the Kent Hall was at risk of being attended by unknown kids.

The Kent Hall was in town just under the market buildings. These were a row of boutique type shops that sold cake making tools, a woman's shoe shop and a hairdresser's. The actual Kent Hall was attached to the Hazlitt Theatre, the place where Mike Reid had once asked Loz for directions to. It was used for children's parties, council meetings, the occasional band and clairvoyants.

Loz and his friends left the playground and within ten minutes had joined the long queue. There were more faces that Loz did not recognise than he did. Kids seemed to be visiting from every corner of the town. Loz knew this was going to be a disco unlike he had ever been to before. He held Theresa's hand tightly ensuring all new comers knew that she was his. He stood as tall and proud as he could in his new tracksuit. Gary stood behind him in his corduroy hooded jacket and flares and Reece in a yellow tee shirt. Robert, Paul, Neil and the others mixed their Mod togs with pastel jumpers and trainers.

The queue edged forward as the Kent Hall doors opened at seven thirty. One of Loz's friends whose name was also Paul asked if he could jump the queue and stand with him. Loz agreed. He liked Paul. He was always cheerful but he had a wild streak in him. Loz had once helped Paul and his dad fix some concrete post in their garden. After their days graft Paul's dad invited Loz to return to their house. The older man poured Loz and his son whiskey and enjoyed being around the young blood and the vigour of youth.

Loz and Theresa squeezed through the door, paid their entrance money and climbed the carpet stairs that led to the main room. *'Cruel summer'* by Bananarama was blaring out of the speakers. The room was large and square shape with long thick wine Red curtains draped from the ceiling to the floor. There was a separate room with a bar that sold only fizzy drinks and crisps. The wooden dancefloor filled quickly with girls dancing to Kool And The Gang, Prince and Ray Parker Junior.

Loz bought a coke for himself and Theresa and stood near the entrance way to the bar. There was a definite sense of excitement and freshness in the air. It was possible that some of these youths had never been to a disco before. As Loz sipped his coke he spotted Nip and Steve trying to chat up two girls in 'Frankie Says' tee shirts. They were trying to be aloof but it obvious they liked the attention. Loz thought it was only a matter of time before Steve unzips his trousers and pokes his shirt through the gap.

'So, you start Monday then do you?' asked Gary. He sounded very northern. Loz was sure that his wedge had grown an extra two inches since their day in Chatham. He compared it to Reece's flick and it too looked much longer.

'Yep, Monday morning at eight.' Said Loz and then added 'It's a fucking piss take though only getting paid twenty seven pounds and fifty pence'

'It's what I get down Top Man and I have to work on Saturday's. You don't have to work on Saturdays do you?' complained Reece.

'Anyway what about you?' asked Loz looking at Gary who was shuffling his feet to some Hip Hop record.

'I've got a job to. It's at a bank. Well not exactly a bank but it's a place where they count the money.'

'So what do you have to do?'.

'My job is to stand by a machine all day and feed thousands of one and five pound notes into the machine and it counts them' Gary informed.

'That sounds really fucking boring' said Loz.

'I know' replied Gary.

'Here do you two have to give your mum's any keep? My mum is demanding five pounds out of my wages and week' moaned Loz.

'Yeah me too,' added Reece.

'Nope, my mum hasn't said anything yet' said Gary.

'That's typical' said Loz 'And I bet your getting more money than us. Did you say you were on the Y.T.S as well?

'No mate, it's not the Y.T.S I'm not working all week for only twenty seven pounds and fifty fucking pence.'

With that he three boy's conversation dried up and Gary walked onto the dancefloor and began to body pop. Reece walked off to the toilets. Robert and Loz smiled at each other and Theresa kissed him on the cheek before she went disappearing into the dark disco to find her friends.

Loz noticed that every other male seemed to be wearing football casual clothes. It was then that he realized that the look was here to stay. He felt good in himself. He liked the clothes he was wearing and he liked the girl who had been swaying on his arm. He accepted then that he was no longer a school boy but would soon be a working boy. He was no longer a Mod but a Casual and he was no longer alone. He listened to the new music playing and thought of Den, Mark, Barry, Malc, Gus and Chelsea and he thought about his new best friends Gary and Reece. His closest and oldest friend Robert stood by his side. Loz felt like his future was looking bright.

'Do you want another coke?' asked Robert nudging Loz on his arm.

'Yea go on then. Can you get some Skips too?'

Robert grinned and walked away. Loz stood alone but he didn't feel alone. Then as if by some magical request the Dee jay changed his music policy and removed the Hip Hop he had been playing. A familiar song began and a massive smile formed over Loz's face. He tapped his foot in time with the record and happily mouthed the words…………

'TRUE IS THE DREAM…………'

SUMMER OF LOVE 1989

RIDE ON TIME

Loz burst into his sister's old bedroom that had now become his brothers since his sister had moved in with her boyfriend six months earlier.

'Where the fuck is my new bottle of aftershave?' Loz demanded.

Loz's brother was lying flat out on his bed reading the sleeve notes on a Mad Professor album. The deep dub reggae record played in the background. Loz glanced around the bedroom thinking how different it now looked since his sister had 'buggered off'. The smell of hairspray, curling tongs and perfume had been replaced with aftershave and sweat. The Human League and Wham records swept aside and UB40 and Bob Marley records lay against the wall instead.

'Erm, I don't know I haven't touched your bloody aftershave.'

'Well somebody has. That aftershave is fucking expensive' Loz yelled.

'I haven't touched it. Ask dad.'

'Dad is hardly going to splash himself with designer aftershave to go up the Civil is he?' tutted Loz and then ran downstairs.

His parents were sitting in the front room laughing at *Blankety Blank* and sharing a chocolate orange. Loz froze on the spot engrossed in the television programme before he remembered why he was there.

'Dad'.

'Yes'.

'Have you moved my Joop by mistake?' quizzed Loz.

'Yes boy, it's nice and it's in my bedroom'.

Loz screwed his nose up then raced upto his parent's bedroom and retrieved the aftershave. He squirted a few drops on his neck whilst running to his bedroom and replaced the aftershave where it should have been, which was next to his record player. He then grabbed his tobacco pouch and ran back downstairs, through the living room and left his parents behind who were still laughing at the show on the tele.

Loz walked down his street. It was like the 'Mary Celeste'. There were no children playing on the steps of the 'Home Brew' centre or the hairdressers opposite that had now closed and reopened as an accountant's. At the bottom of the street he glanced at the corner shop. It was also closed and the building looked abandoned and neglected.

Loz walked along the pavement that was parallel with the Prison wall. It sounded silent inside the Prison walls. He crossed the Boxley Road and passed the George pub. There were two unsavoury looking characters smoking outside who glared at Loz as he passed them. He thought he heard them taking the piss out of his Timbers boots but he carried on walking towards his destination.

Loz knocked on a door on Holland Road where Reece was living in a bedsit. One of the other residents who lived in the bedsit upstairs opened the door. She had long brown scruffy hair and was clutching a Pot Noodle. The smell of it caused Loz to wince. The girl recognised Loz from previous visits so allowed him to enter. He nodded a thank you and entered, then knocked on the first door that he came to.

The door swung open and the stench of hashish washed over Loz. Reece was looking thinner than usual. He wore dirty black jeans and a tee shirt with a picture of the indie band The Dentists on it. Loz stepped into the room uninvited but Reece didn't protest. The room was tiny and smelly and Reece's old sofa bed lent against one of the wall's looking even more battered and bruised than it had five years earlier. The old empty wine bottles with candles sticking out of them had moved with Reece and were scattered around the room.

'What is this you're playing?' asked Loz.

'*Joe's Garage* by Frank Zappa' he replied.

'Weird, but I like it. So what have you been up to?'

'I lost my job at Top Man so I went down the Albion with Steve and got pissed.' answered Reece.

'Right. I'll see Steve tomorrow coz he is coming to his first rave with us.'

'Yeah he did slur something to that effect down the Bin. Where is the rave?'

'Dunno mate, as usual we will have to tune into Centre force and listen out for the meeting points. Will probably be South Mimms or some other service station like that.' Loz informed.

Loz sat on the tatty sofa whilst Reece went off for the kitchen to make some tea. On the floor was a scattered collection of records and books by Stephen King. On one of the record sleeves was a ripped open packet of Rizla and small mound of tobacco. A clipper lighter lay beside a small dark brown lump that looked like a piece of compressed mud.

Reece returned holding two mugs of tea. He drank from his Ipswich Town football club mug whilst Loz sipped from a plain white one.

'So are you going to sign on then?' asked Loz.

'Not just yet. I'm going to the job centre on Monday to see what's on offer. My mum said there's a new building opening that some insurance firm is moving into. She told me that they are looking to employ staff.'

'But you don't know anything about selling insurance' remarked Loz.

'I know but they may have other jobs. There might be something in the post room. Besides it will be nice to not have to work on Saturdays anymore.'

'Are you still thinking about going to University? I remember you mentioned something along those lines months ago.'

'Some days I think it's a good idea and then other days I think it's a stupid idea. I like the idea of attending some university in Manchester or say Brighton and hanging out with the student types but I don't fancy the studying' said Reece.

'You know what I reckon you will enrol somewhere. All that lazying about soaking up the student lifestyle will suit you. You're going to be missed though if it means you have to go up north.'

Reece agreed.

'Look I've got to shoot off coz I'm meeting Gary and the other's down the car park to sort out the arrangements for the rave tomoz, so I'll pop around in the week okay.'

Loz handed his half empty mug of tea back to Reece and they said their goodbyes before Loz saw himself out and headed off in the direction of the car park.

As Loz marched down the road he adjusted his pony tail that was poking through the gap in the back of his baseball cap. He pulled the pony tail tight several times until it felt comfortable again. He then navigated the main road without any danger and walked the few feet towards the car park. Loz could see a white Vauxhall GTE, a navy blue Renault 5 GT Turbo and a red Ford Sierra. There were several people sitting either in the cars or leaning against them. As Loz got nearer he could hear music coming from one of the cars. Loz instantly recognised the tune as the house track *Ride on time'*. The bass, the hi-hats and the pace of the song washed over him and the screaming voice of the singer lifted Loz's mood. He loved the song and had observed it deliver core house music to the masses over the past few months.

Gary noticed Loz approach and waved at him. He was wearing a baggy yellow sweatshirt with 'Champions' written boldly over the chest. On his feet he wore purple Wallabees. Gary punched his hands into the air in time with the music and grinned at Loz. Standing beside him was a short young man whose name was Colin. He had a large mop of hair with a centre parting which meant the fringe hung down like curtains. Colin bounced on the spot as if sitting on an invisible space hopper. The sight of his two friends dancing bought a smile to Loz's face.

'Oi oi.' cried Gary.

'Alright mate' replied Loz.

'How's it going Loz man?' sang Colin cheerfully.

'Yeah good Col. You?'

'Sound mate, sound,' he replied.

'What are you tuned into Sunriser or Centre forcer?' asked Loz.

'88.8 and they're playing some banging toooonnnsssss, you know the score hard core,' said Gary.

'Have they put a shout out yet for the raves happening tomorrow?'

'Yep, they have mentioned a few raves called Biology, Energy and there are a few warm up's in Brixton to. But as always they will not start announcing meeting points until tomorrow night' said Colin.

Loz nodded and rolled a fag. Another two cars arrived in the car park. The first was a silver Fiesta and this was closely followed by a red Metro. The two cars parked alongside the others and people started to jump out of them. Gary leaned inside his Vauxhall and turned the dial up on the radio so he could hear *'S'Express'* better. He punched more fists into the air mouthing the words *'enjoy this trip'* and Colin bounced more vigorously on his invisible space hopper. Loz was still rolling his fag as he approached the red Metro. The driver and front seat passenger had remained in the car. The driver was his friend Steve from school. Loz noticed he was wearing tracksuit bottoms so he wouldn't be doing his shirt through the zipper performance tonight. Steve also sported a large mop of hair with a centre parting and floppy curtains. He was beautifully tanned having spent weeks working on roof tops.

'Alright Steve, are you raving tomorrow?' asked Loz.

'Does a Nun munch carpets?' he replied.

Loz laughed.

'Alright Chang,' said Loz leaning through the cars open window.

Chang nodded. Chang was new to their gang. He was a couple of years younger than Loz and Steve and had only recently been introduced to them via a mutual friend of theirs called Nods. Chang was short and had longish wavy dark hair with a centre parting.

'Are you both thinking of going to that weekender up North somewhere?' Loz asked.

'Kaos. Yeah they keep shouting about it on the pirate radio stations. I think it's going to be in Great Yarmouth' said Steve.

'I heard it's in a Pontins camp in Prestatyn' Chang added.

The three boys shrugged their shoulders. They didn't really care where it was they just knew they would be going. Steve and Chang sorted themselves out and stepped out of the car. The three of them walked back over to Gary and Colin who had now been joined with other young males from the other cars. There was Chris, Justin, Tim, Jason, Smitty and Nods. Another car entered the car park and it caught the attention of the boys. They watched on with curiosity at the car because they did not recognise it. The car slowly pulled up alongside the boots of the over cars and wound down its darkened window.

Steve recognised the driver and walked over to talk to him. The others feeling assured that the driver posed no threat continued with their own car park party. The car stayed for a few more minutes before spinning off. Steve re-joined the group and sided up to Loz.

'Who was that then mate?' asked Gary.

'He is one of the roofers working on the same sight as me at the moment up in Bromley. He is good mates with Matty and Rusty. Did you notice his bird sitting in the front?'

Steve directed the question towards Loz. Loz wondered why Steve had asked him the question and then shook his head.

'Theresa' said Steve.

Loz had not seen Theresa since they had split up a year earlier. He knew he still had a soft spot for her and a part of him wished they were still a couple. But the previous two years had been difficult for Theresa. Loz had spent more and more time going to Chelsea games and she didn't approve of this. Loz had also started to befriend new people that were into the new Acid House dance scene and she didn't approve of this either. Their relationship was doomed for failure. Loz needed to experience life, music, fashion and the new rave scene. Theresa just wanted cozy nights in in front of the idiot box and go to the pictures occasionally. This was not enough for Loz and gradually their relationship crumbled.

Loz accepted that it would only be a matter of time before she or he found themselves in new relationships but now that he discovered that she was it hurt him. It didn't help that he had not met or gone out with anybody since their relationship ended. Gary noticed Loz's pain and stepped in.

'Cheer up mate, it's not all gone Pete Tong yet.'

'I know, I'm alright. Anyway are we still going up to London tomorrow to get our Sunrise membership cards?' asked Loz.

'Sure am. Col was going to come to but now says he cannot come so it will just be you and me.'

'Yeah alright! What time do you want to set off?'

'Eleven. I'll drive straight to the Sunriser shop in Islington then after that we will go to the Booty store in the Kings Road and then we will nip down to Mush on Oxford Street, okay.'

'What do all that and still have time to be ready to rave on in the evening?' cried Loz.

'Yes of course you twat. We will meet up with the others here in the car park at eight and set off to find a meeting point.'

Loz accepted it was going to be a long day but they did need to go to London. They both wanted to buy Sunriser membership cards so that they could join the elite ravers and also access their raves easier. They both wanted to get a pair of desert boots that the Londoners were wearing and the only place they could get them was from a shop in the Kings Road. Loz was not fussed about going to Mush but Gary had his eye on some shirt made of a strange Indian fabric. The style was not yet Loz's cup of tea.

Over the next hour more cars arrived at the car park and others left. Loz stayed until ten thirty and then went home. He decided that he would try and get a good night sleep before his big day in the City. Loz jumped into the rear of Steve's Metro and got a lift home.

Once home Loz found his dad asleep in the front room. The television was still on. Loz slipped passed him without waking him and quietly walked to his bedroom. His mum and brother were asleep. Loz sat on the edge of his bed and untied the laces on his Timberlands reminding himself that another payment on them was due. He had bought the boots on tick from the Army and Navy and had to pay three pounds every month. They were worth every penny though because he loved them. They were the best boots to walk in, dance in and rave in.

He slipped the boots off and shoved them under his bed. Next he removed his baseball cap and pulled the hair band out of his pony tail. It hurt on the way off. He shook his long main of hair thinking to himself that on a good day his hair really could look like Jim Morrison's. Loz then removed the rest of his clothes and got into bed. He deliberately left the sky light blind open so that he could see the stars. He felt a rush of excitement as he told himself that the following night he would again be looking up at the night sky. Only this time it would be at some rave in some field somewhere in one of the Home Counties.

CAN YOU FEEL IT

Before taking himself in hand Loz rolled over and switched on his Hi-Fi system. He reached across further and picked up a tape that Gary had recorded some house tunes onto for him. Loz rubbed the sleep from his blurry eyes and read down the track list. Number one *'Can you feel it'* by Mr Fingers, number two *'Move your body'* by Marshall Jefferson. Loz pushed the tape into the tape deck and pressed play. The thud, thud, thud sound of the Bass drum beat began along with the stimulating chanting of *'Can you feel it'*. Loz sunk back into his bed and slid his hand under the bed sheet. His heartbeat raced and fell into time with the song. A few beads of sweat formed on his forehead. His heartbeat was still rising when the next record started. The fresh sounding piano intro of *'Move your body'* helped to excite Loz even more and then the boom boom boom of the bass drum kicked in. Loz was on his way.

With the job done Loz lay panting on his sweaty bed sheets. He turned his head and saw a pile of flyers for raves. He picked them up and flicked through them. Each of the flyers triggered another memory. He had not even been successful in reaching all of the raves advertised on the flyers. Getting to a rave was a work of art and a skill. It required determination and perseverance and something to help you get through the night.

Loz and his friends had spent hours driving through country lanes in places he had never heard of in convoys. The trick was to evade the Police but keep up with the car in front. The Police would try everything to deny the ravers raving and on more than one occasion they closed the Dartford Tunnel to any cars full of wide eyed youths.

On the top of the pile was a colourful flyer full of psychedelic imagery. It had the words 'Midsummers night dream' written on it and was a rave promoted by the pirate radio station Sunriser. The next flyer was also colourful and had Biology written on it, the next advertised Back to the future, the next Raindance, the next for Loz's first field party in Wrotham called Karma Sutra and the last one Loz looked at before he got bored with looking said Freedom.

Loz dropped the flyers onto the floor and was transported back to his first warehouse party. A year earlier at the end of spring Loz and three friends Stacey, Dave and Rachael had decided to go and visit Rachel's boyfriend Nath down near Portsmouth. They took Dave's Ford Escort estate. They would also sleep in it. Four skinny youthful bodies squashed together like sardines in a tin. Once they met up with Nath he told them about this new type of Acid House parties and all the Dee jay's played was music called Acid House.

Ned knew the location of the Acid House party and in the evening they drove to a warehouse somewhere off the motorway back to London. Loz never knew exactly where they were. Ned knew a few people who at the party and a large group of them entered the inside of the warehouse. It was massive inside and Loz had never seen so many bodies dancing together in one place at one time.

The venue was awash with fluorescent yellow paint on the walls and doors. There were banners with yellow smiley faces on them and many of the revellers wore tee shirts with the same imagery of the smiling face on them. That party was also the first time that Loz saw kids wearing white gloves, bandanas and blowing whistles with such enthusiasm.

It was also the first time Loz saw a generation of kids tripping on aceeeeeeeeeeed. Loz along with a few thousand other teenagers recognised that something fresh and new was in the air. That party had ushered in a new era for Loz and his friends and it was only just the beginning. After that night Loz threw himself into the acid house. He went to Black Box Records in London to buy up the latest releases and frequented shops that he learned sold acid house clobber. He never wore white gloves or a bandana though.

There was one more salient recollection from that particular party. At some point during the night Loz had found himself separated from his friends. He was a little drunk and so found a spot so that he could stand with his back to the wall. Throughout the ten minutes that he stood there he was approached three times by young men dressed from top to bottom in dungarees and smiley tee shirts who asked him if he wanted to buy any trips.

Loz had been amazed by the sheer audacity of it. Illegal drugs were being openly sold by less than obvious kids. The dealers were not the scruffy dishevelled types that Zamo from *Grange Hill* had warned a generation of. These new dealers were ordinary kids who were simply cashing in and helping the fresh new movement to reach greater heights and thousands of more kids.

Once Loz had emerged from his trip down memory lane he got dressed and went down to the kitchen. The house was empty. His mum and dad had left a note on one of the kitchen surfaces where the soda stream maker used to be kept until it was re-boxed and tucked away at the back of one of the cupboards. Loz read the note and it said that they had gone to buy some wallpaper because they were going to re-decorate the front room.

The note also asked if he would be available to help out the following day. Loz threw the note back down thinking to himself that there was no way he would be in a fit state to help out in the morning. After all if he managed to get to a rave he would be leaving the rave when the sun came up and so would not be home until nine at the earliest. There had already been several encounters with family member's preparing their breakfast's whilst Loz was only just returning home. His sister always looked him up and down with suspicion.

Loz lifted the lid on the bread bin and removed a large crusty bloomer. The bread was always extra crusty because whenever his mum would buy bread the first thing she would do was put it in the oven for a while to make it go more crusty. Loz awkwardly cut three moderate slices and spread margarine on them. He flicked the switch on the kettle and waited for it to boil whilst plopping a tea bag into his favourite blue mug.

Once the tea was made he plonked himself down on the kitchen table and unfolded the newspaper that had been left on it. His eyes widened as he caught sight of the headline on the front page *'Ravers cause havoc'*. Loz began to read the article. It had been written by a certain journalist who had evidently made it his mission in life to destroy the empires being built by the promoters of raves. The article suggested that the promoters were linked to the East End London criminal underworld fraternity. It said the criminals were using the illegal parties to traffic their drugs and make drug addicts of a generation. The journalist even went as far as to say that the pirate radio station Centre forcer was being run by members of the notorious Inter-City firm. Loz flung the newspaper onto the table cursing the journalist. Loz assumed his parents had already read the paper so it was too late to burn it.

Loz gulped his tea down and ran up to the bathroom. He was trying something new which meant brushing his teeth after having breakfast. For years his routine involved waking up, getting out of bed, head straight to the bathroom for a wee and then he would brush his teeth. About a week earlier it occurred to him why didn't he brush his teeth after he ate his breakfast? This way his tea and cereal wouldn't taste minty. It was an eureka moment for him and he intended to stick to the new routine. After brushing his teeth he grabbed his wallet and waited by the window to catch the arrival of Gary's car.

PROMISED LAND

Loz got impatient waiting for Gary who was running late. Loz was never late for anything. If anything he annoyed people because he would often turn up earlier than the agreed time. Loz was aware that his turning up early could cause irritation in others but he continued to do it. He told himself that if his friends liked him then they should tolerate this character trait in him. After all it was not like his friends were perfect. But being late was up near the top of Loz's list of things he did not like. Being tired and being sick and racism were also on his list.

Loz huffed before looking out if the window again and picked up the *Radio Times*. He idly flicked through the glossy pages until a film title caught his eye. *'The Amazing Mr Blunden'* Loz and his family had spent many Sunday afternoons watching the film. Loz had a soft spot for it and considered it to be one of the greatest ghost films ever made. He certainly preferred it over the gory Hammer House films.

Loz turned the next page and screwed his nose up at picture of Tuffty the Squirrel. The Squirrel haunted Loz like an unwanted ghost. When he was six years old the primary school he attended called St Pauls sent a letter to his mum informing her that in their opinion Loz was falling behind with his reading skills. As a consequence Loz was forced to attend after school lessons with the woman who lived next door. She had apparently been a teacher before being a house wife became her new job.

For months Loz had to sit in the neighbour's front room and suffer more reading classes. The thing that irritated Loz the most however was that his only recollection of those lessons was that the woman made him read Tuffty the 'Fucking' Squirrel over and over again. Loz vowed he if he ever had a son or daughter he would never make them read anything about a squirrel called Tuffty.

Gary's car pulled up outside Loz's house so Loz opened the door and stepped out onto the street. The sun was shining brightly. Loz opened the passenger door and was almost knocked over the loud bass sub woofers. Gary was nodding his head in time with the song playing and grinning cheekily. Loz slid onto the passenger seat and Gary sped off down the road.

'What do think of this?' he shouted over the music.

'I love it' Loz yelled back 'It's *Fools Gold* by The Stone Roses. It is brilliant isnt it?'

Loz really did love the song and the band behind it. Loz's friend Rich who everybody called Petal even though he didn't like it had raved about the song and the band for weeks. Petal also directed Loz towards another band from Manchester making indie come rave music. The band's name was The Happy Mondays. Loz had bought a couple of twelve inch records by both bands and played them endlessly.

There was even talk of Loz and some of his friends going to a Stone Roses gig at some venue near Liverpool called Spike Island. The idea was that a group of them would jump in a works van, go to the gig and afterwards head to Manchester and check out for themselves what the club the Hacienda had to offer. Loz was keen on the idea it just needed somebody to organise it and get the tickets which would be in demand.

Gary put his foot down and before long they were racing up the M20 towards London at ninety miles an hour. Loz enjoyed Gary's driving. Out of all of his friends that drove Gary was the only one Loz really trusted when it came to driving skillfully. Gary did take risks but he always appeared to be in control. Loz assured himself he was in safe hands and put Gary's skills down to the fact that he drove all day and every day. Gary had been working as a sales representative since losing his job at the Bank. Gary's job meant he spent a great deal of his time with potential customers in London to, so that meant he knew his way around the city.

Gary was having a Madchester session and their motorway journey was supported by songs from The Happy Mondays, Stone Roses, The Charlatans and an assortment of Hacienda house classics like *Voodoo Ray*'. It was only when they came out of the other side of the Blackwall tunnel that Gary removed the tape had been playing and tuned the radio in to 88.3.

The reception was not brilliant and they were surprised that there was even a Dee jay playing this early in the morning. Loz assumed the Dee jay had been doing the nightshift with a little help. Gary tweaked the tuning nob and the Dee jays voice faded in 'A big shout going out for the South Ockenden crew'. Then the voice disappeared for a few seconds. Loz and Gary waited patiently and when the reception regained some strength Adamski's *NRG*' was playing. Loz and Gary danced their hands in the air as if moulding some invisible square box.

The car drove at a snails pace through Hackney and up through Stoke Newington before Gary took one of his short cuts through council estates and narrow streets lined with Georgian terrace houses. They sat in traffic near the Highbury Corner and watched the 'Gooners' strutting arrogantly towards their ground. Gary considered running a couple of them over but instead took another short cut and before long they were parked up opposite the Sunriser shop on Islington High Street.

Both young men marched excitedly towards the shop. They had one intention on their minds. They had decided to buy membership cards for the Sunriser raves and club nights. There were several people around town flashing their membership cards and bragging about getting the heads up earlier than everybody else for the raves happening. Apparently the membership cards also ensured entry and at a reduced fee. Loz found it difficult to believe the reduced fee bit though because rave promoters were making a mint out of young ravers as it was so didn't need to reduce entry fees.

Gary stepped through the shop door first. It was decorated in bright colours. Mostly passionate colours like reds and oranges. There were racks of tee shirts promoting Sunriser raves. Sunriser pirate radio was playing from a large stereo behind the counter. There was one closed door and Loz overheard a couple of ravers saying that behind the doors was where the club was. One of the ravers bragged that he had been inside and said that there were two rooms. The type of membership you had determined what room the raver was allowed into. Loz found this bit curious and he had not heard anything to this effect from those who had been flashing their cards back in his town.

Gary was tempted to buy one of the tee shirts and held several up for Loz's approval. Loz shook his head at each one of them. The shop got fuller as a dozen more ravers dressed in their Timbers and sporting their long wavey pony tails entered. Gary nodded to the counter and edged his way towards it. Loz followed. The surface of the counter was littered with flyers advertising raves.

There were several Sunrsiser raves with colourful psychedelic images of faces and planets. Loz read the flyers whilst Gary started a conversation with the pretty girl working behind the counter. The flyers advertised raves called 'Back to the future part 5' or 'Biology'. At the raves were going be fair ground rides, food and water stalls and a Dee Jay list that named the likes of Grooverider, Paul Trouble Anderson, Paul Oakenfold and Carl Cox. The flyers also boasted rig systems so powerful that they guaranteed to keep each villager awake in their beds from Saturday noon to noon on Sunday. Loz was still admiring the art work and designs on the flyers when his ears suddenly pricked up.

'How fucking much?' cried Loz.

'Twenty quid or thirty quid' Gary answered.

'Twenty quid or thirty quid for just the membership card'.

The pretty girl behind the counter did not look impressed with his outburst. She frowned at Loz whilst she continued to chew on her gum. She wore big gold hoop earing's and had her hair tied back into a pony tail that dangled out of the gap of her red baseball cap that had Sunriser emblazoned on it. The girl also wore a white velour tracksuit. Loz paused from venting his spleen for a moment to suck in the pretty vision. She instantly reminded him of a girl he once watched at a warehouse party. Loz couldn't remember where that party was but he remembered the image of a stunningly attractive girl dressed from top to bottom in a white tracksuit dancing high up on top of a collection of speakers. Everything about that girl had been amazing. Loz was still replaying the image of that girl when the girl behind the counter asked them again if they wanted to buy the membership cards or not. Loz sighed and handed the girl two ten pound notes.

'You don't want to do the thirty pound memberships then?' asked Gary.

'Not particularly, no.'

Loz turned to the girl and asked her what the difference in the memberships was. The girl held up both hands. Between her thumb and index finger on one hand she dangled a gold plastic membership card and in the other hand she waved a red plastic membership card.

'I take it the twenty pound membership is the red card?' Loz assumed.

'What does the gold get us?' asked Gary fondling three ten pound notes.

The girl went on to explain the difference and her spiel didn't take long. Gary looked at Loz and Loz shrugged his shoulders. With that Gary handed the girl twenty pounds. The cards were credit card size and slotted into their wallets easily. Both of them then grabbed a handful of flyers and stuffed them into their tracksuit bottom pockets before leaving the shop. Loz felt like he just wasted twenty pounds.

Loz read out the details of the parties advertised on the flyers as Gary drove through the city on their way to the Kings Road of West London. The streets were mostly full of tourists making their ways to the historical sites of London like 'Big Ben' or the 'Tower Of London'.

'Did you know that the Big Ben that you can see in front of us is not the actual Big Ben at all' started Gary..

'This is Rich aint it a northerner trying to educate a southerner on the historical sites of the nation's capital.'

'So what is Big Ben then?'

'The tower ain't it or perhaps the bloke that built it' returned Loz.

Gary giggled 'No it's the name of the bell inside. The bell that chimes on the hour, you know the one on the nine o clock news is the bell inside the tower not the tower itself.'

Loz looked at Gary and then at the tower. He had to admit Gary had taught himself something there. Loz then read out the details on one particular flyer. It had the words Kaos written on it.

'One of these flyers is for the Kaos weekender. Did we do a Kaos rave once? Anyway it says the dates will be announced soon but it will be three days and two nights on a holiday camp somewhere. Can you imagine that will be a mad weekend.'

Loz liked the idea of a rave weekender. It sounded like a lot of fun and it seemed that most of his friends were intending to go to it. Loz had never done any kind of a weekender. Only two weeks earlier he had bumped into Den, Mark and Baz. They pulled up alongside him on scruffy looking scooters which had the panels cut down on them. The engines panels were also missing so the engine was exposed.

Loz had been pleased to see them as he had not seen much of any of them for the past two years. Den and Mark had stopped going to football in nineteen eighty six just as the hooligan culture was being crushed by the government and the firms were turning their hands to acid house parties rather than terrace battles. Den and Marks substitute was to get back involved with scooter riding and the scooter boy weekenders. Baz had also returned to scooter riding and also raved about as new

Mod band picking up momentum called The Clique. But it had been the stories of their scooter weekenders in Great Yarmouth, Hastings and on the Isle of White really excited Loz.

'Are you going to try to come to the Kaos weekender? It's just that you don't seem to be that excited about the idea of it' asked Loz.

'I want to it's just that my bird is not keen on me going away for a weekender. She don't mind the Saturday night raves as long as I'm still in a fit state to see her by Sunday evening but a whole weekend away will drive her mad' answered Gary.

Loz tutted and then returned to reading the flyers. Gary eventually parked the car in a dead end street off of the Kings Road. He said they would have to be quick because he was at risk of getting a parking ticket in that particular street. They jumped out of the car and crossed the Kings Road and entered the Booty store.

The store was full of racks of brightly coloured shoes. To the left were the Wallabees and to the right were the desert boots. The desert boots were all pastel colours like mauves, pinks and light blues. It was the desert boots that they wanted to buy so they made a bee line for them. Gary immediately snatched a purple pair off of the shelf and Loz grabbed a sky blue pair.

'Is that your size? Slip it on quickly if it is' rushed Gary.

Gary was already slipping his foot into the purple desert boots. Loz copied him. The boots looked and felt fabulous. Gary grabbed the attention of the nearest shop worker and requested the other shoe. He also asked if the other shoe that Loz needed also be got too. A few moments later the shop worker returned with two boxes and the other shoes. Gary and Loz bought their desert boots and charged out of the shop and ran to the car. Gary checked to see if he had a ticket but he didn't. They got back into the car and sped off to Oxford Street.

A car parking space was found a few streets away from Oxford Street. Streets like Oxford and Regent held no appeal for Loz. They were big and wide and full of tourists. Plus they were always busy and Loz didn't manage busy streets well. In fact he didn't really feel comfortable in crowds at all. The only two places where Loz tolerated the massive crowds were Stamford Bridge and raves.

Loz had no idea where the shop Mush was so he obediently followed Gary who seemed to know where everything was. Once inside the shop Loz instantly realized that he didn't like anything in the shop. The styles and materials of the clobber was not his thing at all. Gary, however, was in his northern heaven. He tried baggy shirt after baggy shirt on until he made his choice and purchased one item. Loz thought it looked shit on him but he held his tongue. After all he thought to himself what are mate's for?

Just as they were about to leave Mush a young man in his late teens entered the shop. Loz grabbed hold of Gary's shirt sleeve to stop him walking out of the shop. Loz wanted Gary to see the coat that the boy was wearing. The coat looked incredible and was a real head turner. It was a dark blue hooded coat with streaks of orange pushing through the blue. But the colours of the coat were changing as if responding to the heat in the shop. Loz looked up towards the northern oracle.

'What is that coat doing?' asked Loz.

'It's responding to the heat. It's made of a special fabric called fibre optic.'

Loz nodded and continued to marvel at the boy's coat. The boy appeared to know one of the shop workers and they walked over to him and they fell into a conversation. Loz and Gary tried to remain inconspicuous whilst they stared at the coat.

'Watch,' said Gary.

The shop keeper placed they hand onto the sleeve of the boys coat and then removed their hand. A few seconds passed and Loz and Gary watched in awe as the shop keepers hand left its print on the coat in bright orange. It stayed for a few more seconds and then faded. Loz felt like he was witnessing a magic trick and it certainly beat disappearing rabbits.

'That was fucking amazing' Loz cried on the way back to the car. 'I wonder who makes coats like that.'

Gary winked and said 'It's an Italian label called Stone Island. I doubt it will catch on though because their coats are fucking expensive.'

Once back in the car Gary pushed the tape back into the stereo. The inspirational bass line to Frankie Knuckles *'Your Love'* started. Both boys grinned. Loz asked if it was possible if Gary would drive back home via Bromley. He had heard that there was a ski shop there that was selling reasonably priced ski jackets. Gary asked why Loz wanted a ski jacket in the middle of the summer. Loz replied that he had heard some kids at the last rave talking about ski jackets being the look for the forthcoming autumn and winter months.

The detour to Bromley took longer than they anticipated but they eventually found the ski shop and went inside for a look around. There were many ski jackets but they were far from being reasonably priced. Gary complained that they didn't look good any way and he preferred the old casual's choice of thick coats. Loz agreed but a yellow ski jacket with a royal blue lining did catch his eye. He resolved to return to the shop at some point to buy the coat. He imagined himself wearing theyYellow ski coat also dressed in baggy track suit bottoms and his Timberland boots. It's a look he decided he could carry off.

THE SUN RISING

Loz sat in the front room and ate a plate of mash potato and beans off of his plate whilst he balanced the plate on a tray on his lap. He was watching the news on the television along with his mum, dad and younger brother. Each of them was only half-heartedly watching the news due to be so engrossed in their meals. However Loz's attention was drawn to the idiot box as a Police Officer was introduced and began to be interviewed. In between questions from the reporter images of illegal raves flashed onto the screen. Loz wondered how much attention his parents were paying as the Police Officer criticised the irresponsible ravers who invaded the sedate country sides on the edges of the nation's capital city.

The Police Officer went on to describe the carnage left behind by the ravers and the invasion of peoples good night's sleep. He also mentioned the impact on wildlife; the new drug sweeping through every town, hamlet and city in the United Kingdom called Ecstasy. More footage of raves showed wide eyed young people bopping to the trance like music in dry iced filled venues whilst impressive visuals splashed their lights across them. Everything about the images felt familiar to Loz and he congratulated himself on being a successful raver who also contributed to the second 'summer of love'.

Loz woofed down the last of his mash potato and left the moaning Policeman to the unsuspecting public who didn't really give a shit anyway. After all the British weather in summer time would only support raves in fields for a maximum of three or four months. After that the rave promoters would be seeking out disused warehouses to keep the revellers content.

Loz took his tray down into the kitchen and washed his plate up. Before he ran upstairs to his bedroom he grabbed one of his mum's homemade rock cakes. It had been a choice between the rock cakes or a bowl of ice cream. Loz stood in in front of his wardrobe mirror and brushed his long hair before shaping it into a pony tail and tying it back. He then placed his favourite baseball cap onto his head and pulled the pony tail through it. He admired himself in his new tee shirt with the image of a smiley face within a golden sun. The material shimmered as he swished about. He then put on his Timbers, grabbed some money and raced down stairs, through the front room and out of the front door yelling back 'See you later.'

Loz decided to take a slightly longer route to the car park. He had an urge to walk along the alley way beside the Howard Wardell youth club. As Loz approached the alley he had a flash back memory of the first time he really spoke to Den the night of the disco on the last day of school. He could picture himself as that younger, naive boy in his Mod gear. He sighed.

Loz peered down into the windows with their tatty metal mesh guards. The basement where he had learnt to dance and snog was dark and quiet. The alley way even seemed filthy and neglected with its scattered beer cans, empty crisp packets and fag buts. The main gates to the youth club were closed and the place looked tired. Loz wondered if Dave was still the manager and realized that he had not stepped into the youth club since the first night he attended the Kent Hall disco. That had been a turning point and from there on a whole new world of girls, friends and music opened up and swallowed him whole. Thank the gods.

The pub at the end of the road also sounded quiet. Loz wondered how his friend Nip was getting on at university. He had run off the year before to acquire a qualification in architecture. Nip also had some notion of living in Hong Kong for a few years too. Loz then considered knocking on Isabel's door but told himself that she would be out with her new boyfriend. She and Baz had been seeing each other for a couple of months. It was still early days but the relationship looked hopeful. Loz then crossed the road and walked through a new tiny kids play area and then he joined the main road that led pass Reece's bedsit. He decided not to disturb him assuming he would be deep into a Doors album and made his way to the car park.

Gary's white Vauxhall was parked alongside Steve's red Metro and three more cars were parked beside Steve. The doors on Gary's car were wide open and Loz could hear the piano and strings building on *'Rhythm is rhythm'*. Loz nodded to the bass drum beat as he shook hands with Gary and then Steve and then the others. Gary was wearing his new Mush clobber and purple desert boots. Steve was also wearing desert boots in a pastel pale green. He wore a bright red long sleeve shirt with golden patterns on it.

'Alright,' came a voice and Loz swung round to see his mate Pedro standing behind him.

'Didn't you hear me calling you? I was walking twenty yards behind you down the road' he said.

'No sorry Pedro mate, I was lost in my own world' Loz apologised.

'Oi what are these stories I'm hearing about your crazy leg dancing session the other night at the Red Lion' laughed Gary.

'Fuck off, it's bollocks. You have the wrong bloke' Pete replied.

There was some teasing and laughter at Pete's alleged crazy dancing at some indoor rave in a venue at the back of some boozer in Gravesend. Loz and his gang sometimes visited the place if they were either skint or couldn't be arsed to go searching the country side for a party.

'What's this I heard about you and a bogey,' Pedro asked Steve.

'What's this then Steve?' Loz added.

'Well you know that my mum and dad are trying to sale their house yeah. Well, this woman came around four times to view the place. She started to piss me off right coz all she would do was complain about something in this room or that room or some other silly bollocks. So the last time she came for another look around I was having my tea in the living room. I was already pissed off about something. Any way I get up and let her in and my mum starts to show her around the house yet again. I can hear again moaning about this and that so I've had enough. I notice she slipped her sandals off left them by the front door. Then I have this idea. I pick a really big and horrible sticky bogey. I mean it even had bits of blood in it and I wipe it on the inside of her sandal and then go and sit back down to finish my tea. I wait for her to come down stairs. She moans a few more times whilst getting nearer to the front door. Eventually she runs out of moans and decides to leave. You should have seen her face as she slipped her foot back into her sandal. Funny as fuck.'

'That is fucking disgusting' said Pedro. The others agreed but were too busy rolling around with laughter. Only Steve could conjure up such a punishment. Two more cars joined the gathering in the car park. Les jumped out of one of the cars and Chang jumped out another and they joined Loz's group. The boys chatted about the plans for the evening and Gary turned the volume up further on his car stereo so they could listen to the announcements on Centre forcer. The Dee jays were suggesting a rave was going to happen somewhere in the Essex country side. That was the in place to be on tonight.

'Did you hear about Brendon?' started Lee 'He got arrested at West Ham for taxing another kid from Spurs. He is up in front of the Magistrates next Tuesday.'

'Nope I have not seen him for ages' said Loz.

'The last I heard he was still nicking designer togs off of peoples washing lines. He has been doing it for years. He once nicked me a Pringle jumper off some poor sods line. I've still got the jumper I think' added Steve.

'Talking about washing lines. I was searching through my wardrobe the other week for my old Fila BJ tracksuit. But I couldn't find it so I ask my mum if she has seen it. Oh yeah she says, I washed it ages ago and it shrunk so I gave it to the charity shop she says. I couldn't believe it. I really liked that tracksuit top' said Chang.

There was more laughter and sorting out arrangements and then the Dee jay revealed that the first meeting point of the night was going to be on Blackheath. Gary announced it was time to be heading off and the crowd of boys dispersed into various cars. Loz, Pedro and Chang jumped into Gary's. Gary led the convoy of adventurers out of the car park up the hill and onto the M20. Seven car loads of ravers in all charged down the motorway in the direction of the meeting point on Blackheath Common.

Each of the seven cars was tuned into Centre forcer radio. The night promised something special and Loz was totally on board. The Centre force Dee jay informed its listeners that Guru Josh was going to be at the rave and that there may be a possible appearance from Adamski with a new singer he is using whose name was Seal. There was argument's in the car because Pedro trying to convince his travelling companions that Adamski's real name was Adam Ski but nobody believed him. The

Dee jay then played more request which he always introduced by yelling 'And a big shout going out to....'

About three miles before they reached Blackheath the Centre forcer Dee jay announced that there was going to be another meeting point at the Black Prince hotel on the A2. Gary changed direction and the six cars behind him followed. Within five minutes of driving at eighty miles an hour Gary steered his car into the Black Prince car park. There a few more cars already there that appeared to have ravers in them. Everybody eyed one another up suspiciously. The other six cars soon followed and parked awkwardly around the car park.

Steve pulled up beside Gary's car and wound down his window. Steve was about to yell something when Loz noticed the smile on his face suddenly disappear. Loz and Gary both looked to see what Steve had spotted. Three Police cars screeched into the car park and one stopped in the entrance way therefore blocking the cars exits. The Police cars surrounded the cars full of ravers and coppers jumped out of their cars and instructed all the drivers to switch off their engines. Gary twisted the tuner on the radio to disguise that he had been listening to Centre force. There were complaints from the drivers but they were ignored as the Police assumed control of the situation.

'Bollocks' said Gary 'They must have intercepted the info about the meeting points.'

'Yes, this could mean an early night for us all' replied a disappointed Loz.

'Yeah trust us to be the first ones here. If we had not of driven so fast we could of spotted the old Bill from the A2' added Chang.

'Can you all step out of the car please lads.' demanded the booming voice of an older Police Officer.

Loz noticed they were Kent Police and not Metropolitan. The four of then slowly got out of the car. The Police Officer asked them to step a few feet away from the car. Loz noticed the same thing was occurring with some of the other cars as Police Officers dived into the cars giving them a thorough search for drugs. One officer pushed and heaved the back seat in Gary's car until he handed out the entire seat. Gary looked like he was going to cry.

'So where arc you lads off to tonight?' asked the copper.

'Just driving around' Gary mumbled.

'Just driving around eh! I don't believe you. I think you have your sights set on going to one of those illegal raves.'

'Not us' Said Pedro.

'You look like ravers to me.'

The copper then nodded towards the other cars in the car park and added 'Your mates look like ravers too.'

There was some more banging and clattering as the Police Officer inside Gary's car did his best to dismantle the interior. Loz and the others kept quiet and tried to look innocent. Another much younger police man worked his way around each raver and asked them to remove all the items in their pockets. Loz grinned at the sight of lighters, Rizlas, tissues, hankerchiefs and chewing gum wrappers. The whole debacle lasted about thirty minutes and then the old Police Officer in charge of the operation announced that everything was okay but advised that they all turned around and drove back down the M20. Loz and the others had no intention of doing so but agreed just so that they could make a quick get and get to Blackheath before everyone else moved on to the next meeting point.

The coppers jumped back into their cars with disappointed faces and drove off. Gary suggested that they wait five minutes before they set off again for Blackheath. They all laughed and joked about their encounter with the rave busters. In the meantime Gary tuned in again to Centre forcer and the Dee jay was still instructing everybody to go to Blackheath. The Dee jay even announced that he had heard that a bust had recently occurred at the Black Prince. Loz's and his mates felt like heroes.

Once Gary was satisfied that the coast was clear he led the charge again out of the car park and down the A2 towards Blackheath. As soon as they exited the A2 the traffic slowed due to the volume of cars heading in the direction of the Common. It took a further ten minutes to reach Blackheath. Everyone in the car was astounded by the sheer volume of cars parked all over the common. Loz estimated that there must have been five hundred cars scattered on the grassy heath.

Gary mounted the curb and skidded towards a space not far from a small roundabout. The rest of their convoy followed suit and they parked in a circle. It reminded Loz of the way the cowboys and their wagons full of their wives, children and belongings used to park in the old Westerns when they were attempting to protect themselves from the savage Red Indians.

Loz jumped out of the car first and the site of the hundreds of ravers eager to get raving excited him. He had been at meeting points before but he had never witnessed anything like this before. It felt great to be a part of it. Police cars parked on the fringes of the Heath and the coppers roamed in amongst the raver's cars wearing their fluorescent overcoats. They glowed in the parked cars headlights. Car after car had its doors wide open and belted out music from the various pirate radio stations. Loz even spotted a few kids dancing on the roofs of their cars. The site was spectacular.

Loz and Gary snaked their way in and out of the cars occasionally chatting to other ravers. The atmosphere was one of anticipation, friendliness and nervous excitement. There were several older males holding brick size mobile phones to their ears. They were part of the organisers of the rave. They were surrounded by ravers asking questions and waiting for information regards the location of the next meeting point or the pot of the gold itself.

'E's, E's' whispered the voice of a young man dressed in yellow dungarees and wearing a red beret on his head. The man weaved his way in and around the waiting ravers. A few seconds later Loz heard another voice advertising purple ohms and black microdots. Loz looked up into the black star lit London sky. It looked still and distant and a universe away from the chaos below on the heath. Loz knew that this was one of the best nights of his life.

'Alright man' boomed a gruff voice and Loz looked to his left to see a familiar face but he couldn't recall from where. Loz shook the man's hand desperately trying to place where he recognised the man from.

'Clinks,' the man revealed, 'You don't remember me do you?'

'Ah yeah, Clinkers, of course' said Loz smiling.

'That was one of the best nights there. Did you have a good one?'

Loz cast his memory back to the last time he went to the Clinkers club down Clinker Street in Southwark. That night had been memorable for two reasons. The first was that on the way into the club the bouncer searched Colin and found a small amount of Hash. Instead of confiscating it all the bouncer tore the hash in half and gave the smaller half back to Colin before allowing him inside. The second salient memory was that the club blew Amyl-nitrate through the club. The effects were horrid and Loz hated the smell of it.

'Do you remember the Amyl?' asked the man and Loz nodded pretending that he found the whole experience awesome. The man then jogged on the spot for a while, screwed his face up and pouted his lips. Loz understood that the man was coming up on an E. The man then mumbled some more things before being called over by his mates.

There appeared to be some instructions about another meeting point from the men with their mobile phones. Ravers started to jump into the cars and dart this way and that attempting to find and follow the leader. Loz and Gary raced back to their vehicle and jumped inside. Like a well drilled military operation all the ravers returned to the cars with haste and joined the massive convoy. The Police did their best to ascertain what was happening and keep up.

'What's the word?' Loz asked Gary.

'The word is there is another meeting point at the South Ockendon service station.'

'Where the fuck is that?' moaned Pedro.

'It's off the M25 in Essex.' Gary informed before skidding off the grassy common and hitting the tarmac at speed. There was a whoosh of excitement in the car as they followed a green Golf GTE in front of them. Gary turned up the volume on the radio and 808 State rocked the inside of the car.

They drove back down the A20 alongside other cars evidently full of ravers. They merged with the M25 and hurtled down it towards the Dartford tunnel. As they approached the tunnel they noticed that the Police had closed several of the gates in an attempt to prevent the cars full of ravers crossing the Thames and entering Essex and finding their way to the rave. Fortunately Gary swung the car away from the closed gates and they managed to sneak through undetected. Gary bolted through the tunnel along with other successful cars of ravers. As they exited the tunnel they felt confident that they were going to reach the rave intact. Loz was not familiar with the area of Essex but he trusted Gary would find the service station.

On their arrival at the South Ockendon service station they could already see that several cars were leaving. Gary pulled into the service station because he also needed to refuel. It was apparent that they had lost three of their convoy. Gary filled his car with petrol and chatted with the ravers in the car behind who were also filling up with fuel. They informed him that they were from Hertfordshire and that the rave was nearby. Gary relayed the information about the location of the rave to Loz, Chang and Pedro.

Gary had arranged to follow the ravers from Hertfordshire and they set off down the A13. As they left the service station more and more cars of ravers pulled into it. They got the sense that this rave was going to be a massive affair. Gary followed the car in front and Steve followed close on the heels of his bumper behind. They drove through Thurrock and North Stifford until they reached a small village called Orsett. There was a stunned silence inside the car. The adrenalin inside them was buzzing. They sensed the rave was nearby. The hypnotic sounds of 'Sueno Latino' reflected their mood and expectations.

They drove through country lanes which were filled with parked cars. Police officers in the fluorescent glowed as they lined up along a stretch of lane that led to the rave. They reminded Loz of the lights on the run ways in airports. The police had given up trying to deter the cars full of ravers. They had no choice as twenty thousand excited and determined youths caused havoc.

The car in front found a spot big enough to park in and as Gary's car passed them they shouted out 'Have a good one'. Gary slowly drove down the country lane until a youngish Policeman waved them down and instructed Gary to wind down his window. Loz's heart sank assuming they had been busted and would be told to turn around or even worse get arrested. Loz looked at the flashing lights in the sky that were being projected from inside the field where the rave was. He could hear the thumbing deep bass of the house music and was ready to plead with the copper to allow them to continue with their quest. The copper simply told Gary to continue down the lane for another two hundred yards and there he would find a parking space.

Gary and Loz thanked the Policeman and cheered as they drove down the lane. Loz looked out through the rear window and observed at least another fifty cars behind them. He could see Steve in his Metro bouncing around inside as he responded to the music coming from the rave.

Gary found the car spaces and chose a spot. They gathered their coats and jackets and jumped excitedly out of the car. There was a group of men twenty yards in front of them clutching their mobile phones and waving to them to hurry up.

'Well then,' said Loz 'Nice one for getting us here Gary.'

'Piece of piss mate,' he replied.

'So what do you think, twenty quid to get it?'

'Maybe twenty five but look at the size of the rave. It's massive, our biggest yet.'

Loz soaked in the sights and sounds of the rave as they walked nearer to it. They could spot a Ferris wheel and other fairground rides. There were flashing laser lights and psychedelic images being projected all over the site of the rave. Loz prepared himself for the next seven hours of dancing and looked forward to the sun coming up at five and the Dee jays responding to it by playing the Beloved's *'The sun rising.'*

For the final paces before Loz reached the entrance gate he whispered the words from the song. And with that he handed the bouncer twenty pounds and tripped into the rave.

THE END